I0568349

To Love, LOVE

Steve Robinson

Table of Contents

Dedication

In 2013, I was having a hard time finding employment after I was fired from my previous job. My good friend, Maela Way encouraged me to apply for a Play Coach position for the Crenshaw YMCA, located in South Los Angeles. Where her older sister Virgess Way was the sites coordinator. A play coach was a PE teacher for grades; kindergarten to fifth grade. We would go to Tom Bradley Elementary and Hillcrest Elementary and teach them the value of physical education.

I was introduced to a woman by the name of Anna Hurst, who was the Head of School at the charter school on the same campus as Tom Bradley named Libertas College Prep. The school was looking for a PE teacher, and I applied, but they initially wanted to hire one of my coworkers, Bobby Nigg. He did not take the position and then recommended me. In 2014, my journey began as the PE teacher at Libertas College Prep. I had the pleasure of also working with a woman named Allison Metz, who started as the principal of the school the same year I started as the PE teacher. In 2015, after my first year, I was then asked to be the assistant Dean. I can honestly say I didn't see that coming. In 2016, I became the full-time Dean of students. Working with the youth on that level changed my perspective on life. I can't thank Anna Hurst and Allison enough for believing in me and my abilities to build and maintain strong relationships with the students.

I've had the pleasure of inspiring and being inspired by hundreds of students from the ages of five to thirteen. Those experiences I will never take for granted. My inspiration for this book is for those countless students that believed me in. THANK YOU!

Acknowledgments

My mom, Cheryl Denette Robinson, once said to me when I was 16, "Never be afraid to shine your light because it is bright." Her and I were always close; she taught me the value of understanding who I was as an individual. She would often say to me, "Talk to me son." She said that was her way of getting inspired, and sometimes, the things I would say to her would do just that. About a week before she passed away, we had a conversation on the phone and she was extremely adamant about me promising her that I would never drink alcohol or smoke. I can proudly say I have never done either. The light she shined in my life will never be dim. She continues to live within me and my other siblings.

My good brother, Deonse "Dsay" Blackwell, once said, "Rock with how you feel and trust it, EVERY TIME!" This is a friendship that has lasted for two decades. Audubon middle school is where we connected, and we haven't lost connection, not one time. He was the very first person I called when my mom passed away on January 14, 2006. "Momma Monica" (his mom) has been my second mom since then. Dsay is a person that has always put others before himself; he currently manages a place called, Florence Fresh located in Los Angeles, CA. Where he is dedicated to giving opportunities to up and coming businesses to promote their businesses. Momma Monica and Dsay have been a light that has continued to shine in my life. Two people I look to for inspiration.

My good brother, Shaheed Muhammad once said, "Carry yourself knowing that someone is always watching." This is a friendship that has lasted for the past decade. I was introduced to him at Crenshaw high school in Los Angeles, CA. A basketball teammate, friend, and more importantly someone I look to as a brother. He has had the pleasure of working with our youth in Arizona for 10+ years as a behavior counselor. The best way I can describe him is he's a man that values his morals and principles, he stands for something and he doesn't allow anyone to encourage him to lose sight of that. We've been able to see each other's growth from boys to men.

My good brother, Tyrone Nance, once said, "The youth are true manifestations of the foundation we create through our hopes and inspirations." This is a friendship that has lasted for the past decade. Playing basketball at Crenshaw high school is what brought us together. He is now the president of a non-profit organization called, "It's Bigger Than Us", they have been able to do so much for the community, from back pack giveaways, food drives which they do every Friday, and so much more. This is only their second year. The best way I can describe him is he's a man that when he sets his mind and heart to do something he does it and doesn't make excuses as to why he can't. I appreciate that so much. Keep striving for greatness.

My good brother, Marquis Felder, once said, "You're where you supposed to be, you have everything you need, and you know everyone you need to know to reach your goals in life." This friendship has lasted over a decade, we met at Crenshaw high school. We then decided to move to Houston, Texas. In Houston, not only did we become roommates but we became family. We had to depend on one another in ways we couldn't ever imagine. The best way I can describe Marquis is when he gets locked in on anything it is impossible to break his focus. For example, he started his own pizza business, called "pizzaman_la". He has sold over 2,000 pizzas and still counting. He has become the ultimate family man, seeing him with his family is not only inspiring but also encouraging. He speaks life into his loved ones.

My good brother, Denzel Henderson, once said, "If you can make 100 excuses, always plan on having 101 solutions." This friendship began in the 9th grade, he was in a whole new world, transitioning from private school to public school. We recognized one another from the Boys and Girls club in South Central LA. This friendship has lasted over a decade. The best way I can describe Denzel has a profound perspective on life and a steadfast approach to how he enjoys life. Our bond grew even bigger because we both lost our moms at early ages. When we get a chance to talk about our moms, it always brings a smile to my face. I am a firm believer in that our experiences shape who we are and let's just say his experiences developed a way of thinking that is like no one else I know and I value and cherish that a great deal.

About The Author

Steve Robinson, born September 11, 1988, raised in South Central, Los Angeles, CA to parents who both served and met in the army. One of six children, I have three sisters and two brothers. I attended Crenshaw High School and played several sports: basketball, ran track, tennis, and even was a proud participate of the swim team, despite my fear of diving. I had the pleasure of attending the University of Houston were I obtained my Bachelors Degree in Communications in May of 2010. In 2014, I began working with our youth at the YMCA being a Play Coach for one year.

One year later, in 2015, I became a PE teacher for a Charter School in South LA, named Libertas College Prep. At the end of that school year, I was promoted to the Assistant Dean for one year and then became the full time dean. From 2017-2020, I had the pleasure of inspiring and being inspired by our youth in ways I could've never imagined. Writing is my life and has been my life for the past twenty plus years. My goal is to have this book in high school english curriculums.

Chapter One

Jamal Thompson was born and raised in Los Angeles, CA. He lost his dad to brain cancer at the age of twelve, his mom passed away when he was fifteen, and from there, he was raised by his grandmother. His mom and dad split up when he was six; after that, he would split time with them both, with his mom Mondays to Thursdays and his dad Fridays to Sundays. He thought he had a great life; I mean, sure, his mom and dad weren't together, but they still loved each other very much. Ellis is Jamal's best friend, and they met in the first grade; when you saw Jamal, you saw Ellis and vice versa. As kids, they loved to play video games and ride bikes, but most of all, they loved to talk about things they would invest in when they were older. Jamal loved the idea of being able to buy a lot of houses, and Ellis loved the idea of decorating those houses.

All throughout middle school, both boys got really good grades and often made the Honor Roll. Even though they thrived in the classroom, Jamal always saw himself working for himself, and so did Ellis. So much so that during school, they would call each other CEO Jamal and CEO Ellis. Before you know it, they had a crew and called themselves "The CEO Boys". Mr. Bright, the 8th-grade math teacher, got wind of the name of their crew and began to make fun of them, saying, "You guys think just because you call yourselves CEO's then you will magically be one."

That crew consisted of like-minded young men at their middle school, five boys in total; Justin, Paul, and Jason. You can say all five young men were very mature for their ages. From then on, the five boys quickly became inseparable; all were very interested in the idea of real estate and, more importantly, owning it. As young men, they knew one thing, we have to make this more than just a "click". Once all of the young men graduated and moved on to high school, they knew they wouldn't be able to see each other as much because they all were not going to attend the same high school. For instance, Jamal attended a private school in Los Angeles called High Roads Prep, and Ellis also attended the same school. Justin attended Los Angeles City Prep, a public school in Los Angeles, and Paul attended Victory High School, which was a public school as well. Lastly, Jason attended Trinity High School.

Jamal and Ellis made some very strong connections throughout their high school experiences, the main one for Jamal was a young lady by the name of Sabrina, a girl he became very interested in, in their 9th grade English class. Sabrina was a very creative and free spirit, and Jamal was instantly drawn to her. Sabrina is the youngest of three siblings, which in some cases would make you think she was spoiled or always got what she wanted regardless of what it might be. Jamal would consistently contemplate how he would approach Sabrina and often talk himself out of it.

On that day, a very rainy wet day, Sabrina asked Jamal if he could walk her to class because he had an umbrella and she wanted to be protected from the rain. This was Jamal's chance and maybe his only chance, so he asked her, "Do you go with anybody?"

She laughed and replied, "Not at all," she further said, "Why do you ask?"

He nervously replied, "Because I like you, and I was

wondering if you like me too."

She smiled and said, "How do you know you like me?"

He said, "I just know, and when you know, you know."

They entered the class as if the conversation they just had never took place; he sat in his seat, and she sat in her seat. When class ended, he offered to walk her to her locker, but she said, "No thanks." Jamal ran into Ellis in the hallway and was overjoyed with excitement as he could barely gather his words to make a complete sentence.

Ellis said, "Are you alright?"

Jamal replied, "I am better than alright. I talked to my crush today, and she actually talked back."

Sabrina met up with her best friend Mercedes and told her all about her encounter with Jamal. As she was telling Mercedes, she couldn't help but to hesitate and was unsure of Jamal's true interest level. Even though she was unsure, she still was curious and wanted to know more about Jamal and expressed to Mercedes how intrigued she was.

Mercedes said, "I like Jamal. He really seems like a nice guy." As soon as Mercedes finished that sentence, Sabrina began smiling from ear to ear but trying to hide it. "It is okay to like a boy; we are growing up."

Sabrina and Mercedes met in the third grade, and since then, they had been inseparable, similar to Jamal and Ellis. Mercedes was more of a social butterfly and didn't mind the attention from boys. Although she made it clear that this was not her main focus, she still wouldn't discourage it if it came her way. She also had an extreme love for cheerleading and couldn't wait until she was able to try out for the high school team. As the bell rang to end school for the day,

Jamal met up with Ellis so they could catch the bus home. As they began walking, Jamal heard a girl calling his name, "Jamal, Jamal, wait up." Much to his surprise, it was Sabrina.

He stopped and said, "What's up? Do you want to walk with us?"

She said, "No, my mom is waiting on me in front of the school, but I wanted to give you my phone number so you can call me tonight."

Jamal smiled and said, "Definitely!"

As Jamal and Sabrina were talking, Ellis was in the background dancing because he was excited for Sabrina and his best friend, Jamal. Ellis said, "Man, I want my high school crush to track me down and give me her phone number, damn you're lucky."

Jamal said, "I'm not lucky this is the universe, and the universe is undefeated, my friend,"

Ellis replied, "Yea, sure, Jamal." They both laughed in unison.

As they walked to the bus stop, Jamal asked Ellis, "What do you want to do after you graduate from high school?"

Ellis stopped immediately and said, "I want to start my own business and buy as much real estate as I can." Ellis told Jamal he often had dreams of the two of them buying property, having their own company, supporting their loved ones, and also being married with kids and their kids being just as close as he and Jamal were, if not closer.

Jamal looked at Ellis in his eyes and said, "The journey starts now."

As soon as Jamal got home, he began thinking of names for a business for him and Ellis. Overwhelmed with excitement, he then called Ellis and told him, "We have to start thinking of company names. Let's not waste any time."

Ellis said, "Definitely! But let me call you right back after I finish helping my mom."

Jamal said, "Alright, sounds good!"

After Jamal finished his homework, he began pacing back and forth in his room, trying to gather up enough courage to call Sabrina. As he was pacing, his grandma called him into the living room because she wanted to talk to him. Rose began to tell Jamal how proud she was of him and how she saw great things for him in the future. Jamal was listening and wondering why his grandma was saying these things. Of course, it felt good hearing it, but he was very confused as to why she was saying it at this moment.

Jamal said, "Thanks, grandma, but what made you say that?"

Rose said, "I felt like you needed to hear me say it, and I wanted you to know whatever you decide to do, you have my full support."

Jamal said, "Alright, grandma, can I be excused? I have a call to make."

Rose said, "Of course my son, but who do you have to call?"

Jamal just got up from the table and walked fast to his room.

*****

On the car ride home with her mom, Sabrina told her that she had met a boy and expressed to her mom that she might like him. Her mom said, "What is his name, and why do you think you might like him?"

Sabrina said, "While I was walking to class, I saw he had an umbrella, and so I asked if I could walk with him under it. He said, 'Yes! Of course.' From there, we had a conversation, and he was very nice, kind, and respectful, all of the things I remember you telling me to look for in a boy. Much to her mom's surprise, she was happy for her daughter, mainly because she knew what to look for in a boy despite their age.

Once they made it back home, Sabrina anxiously awaited a call from Jamal. Not only was she looking forward to it, she couldn't wait for him to call. To pass the time, she began to clean up her room, and while doing so, she decided to stop and write him a letter, a full-page letter. As she completed the first half of the letter, her phone rang at 5:33 PM, and it was a call from Jamal.

Jamal paced back and forth in his room and began having a talk with himself before he called Sabrina, saying, "You got this. This is something you've wanted since you first saw her!"

He sent a text to his friend Ellis and said, "I'm about to call Sabrina. Wish me luck!"

Ellis responded back and said, "Good luck, bro."

Jamal dialed Sabrina's phone number. The phone rang three times, then Sabrina answered the phone and said, "Hello, took you long enough to call me, Jamal."

Jamal laughed and said, "I had to get my homework done first, but I'm glad you were waiting for my call."

The two began to have a conversation to get to know one another, and that conversation ended at 9:30. Both got off of the phone excited and happy, of course, for different reasons. Jamal was happy because he finally was able to get to know the girl he had been crushing on since the beginning of the high school year. Sabrina was excited because she had no idea Jamal was interested in her and was confused as to why she never paid him any mind. Both Jamal and Sabrina were looking forward to seeing each other at school the next day, and in fact, they even planned to meet each other at a corner so they could walk to school the rest of the way. Sabrina's mom was apprehensive at first, but she did ultimately give in to the idea of them doing so.

While getting ready for school that day, Jamal's grandma noticed he paid a lot more attention to his appearance than usual, so inevitably, she asked him, "Who are you getting so dressed up for?"

Jamal replied, "No one, grandma. I love you, and I'll see you later."

As he walked out of the house, his grandma noticed he had applied a lot of cologne and said to herself, "My son must have a little girlfriend," she laughed and walked back into her room.

Jamal arrived at the location first, and as he patiently waited for Sabrina, he couldn't help but think to himself, "It is actually happening. I'm actually here at this corner waiting on her." Sabrina and her mom slowly pulled up, and Jamal greeted her by opening the door for her and giving her a hug. Then he walked over to the driver's side and introduced himself to Sabrina's mom by saying, "Grand rising Sabrina's mom, my name is Jamal. Nice to meet you."

Sabrina's mom replies, "Well, hello, Jamal, nice to meet you as well, and I apologize for my daughter. I can see she never told you my name." She laughed, "My name is Ms. Oliver."

Jamal smiled and said, "Nice to meet you, Ms. Oliver."

Both Jamal and Sabrina then began walking to school, both

nervous and excited at the same time. Neither one wanted to be the first person to say anything, so they both casually walked until one of their classmates noticed them while driving with their parents and yelled out, "Hey, Sabrina and Jamal."

That seemed to have broken the ice for both of them as Jamal said to Sabrina, "Your mom seems super cool."

Sabrina laughed and replied, "Yea, she is for the most part." Sabrina then asked Jamal, "How cool is your mom?"

Jamal said, "My mom was very cool."

Sabrina paused and said, "Was?"

Jamal said, "She passed away when I was six years old."

Sabrina then gave Jamal the biggest hug she could and apologized. From that moment on, she had a different level of respect for Jamal, not because she felt sorry for him but because she had no idea he had experienced that so young and was in the headspace he was in.

Chapter Two

Ellis began struggling academically because his mom had been in and out of the hospital battling breast cancer. It would go from bad to good, then good back to bad. Ellis hadn't been able to fully get his mind off of it, so much so he had started to become anti-social and had been staying to himself. Jamal was unaware of the hardships Ellis and his family were dealing with. As a matter of fact, Ellis sent a text to Jamal saying, "My mom is the backbone of our family, and I don't know how we would proceed without her."

Jamal responded back and said, "What do you mean, bro?"

Ellis then broke the news to Jamal and said, "I don't know how much longer she's going to be with us. Her breast cancer has resurfaced."

Jamal called him immediately and said, "Are you at home? If so, I'm coming over."

Jamal knew how important it was for him to be as supportive as he possibly could regardless of what capacity that support was in. Once Jamal arrived at Ellis' house, he heard Ellis crying in his room with his head in his pillow. Jamal was unsure of what to do, so he walked into the room and gave his friend a long hug. As he was hugging Ellis, Ellis just slowly began to apply all of his weight onto Jamal as he was beginning to let go of all of his emotion. Once they stopped hugging, Ellis thanked Jamal for being supportive and helping him. As scared and frightened as Ellis was, he still was able to laugh and joke with his good friend Jamal about Sabrina and how they were a match made in heaven. In fact, Ellis had hope that he would be able to find that love in a woman sooner than later.

Homecoming was fast approaching, and Ellis was beginning to feel the pressure of not having a date and not having the courage to ask the girl he liked or had been having a crush on since the beginning of the school year. Her name was Angelica, and she was in the eleventh grade. He first saw her in the hallways walking to class, and he couldn't take his eyes off of her as she was talking to one of her friends. Unfortunately, she didn't notice Ellis, but that didn't stop Ellis from saying to himself, "I have to approach her, she has to know I like her, and I'm interested."

So as it got closer and closer to the two best friends going to their first Homecoming dance, Ellis finally gained the courage to ask Angelica to be his date. He walked up to her and said, "Hello, my name is Ellis, and I was wondering if you were going to homecoming and if you had a date."

She laughed and said, "Yes, I am, and I have a date, and if I didn't, I wouldn't go with you."

Ellis looked at her and said, "Well, alright."

Ellis wasn't even upset by her words or bothered. In fact, he was relieved and was glad he approached her so he could see her personality and not just her physical appearance, which he was initially drawn to. Ellis was debating with himself on if he should tell Jamal about what happened because he didn't know what his response would be. Would Jamal make fun of him? Would he have his back? He truly didn't know. He did decide to tell Jamal, and Jamal responded by saying, "All you can do is try and hope for the best." He also added, "I'm glad you stepped outside of your comfort zone despite how tough it was."

Spirit Week came, which was the name associated with most high schools during homecoming. For all five days, there was a theme attached to each day, Monday was Pajama Day, Tuesday was Favorite Sports Player, Wednesday was Wacky Tacky, Thursday was Dress like twins, and also it was the Girl vs. Girl Flag Football game, which was also known as the "Powderpuff" game, Friday was College Day, students could wear apparel that indicated what college they wanted to attend. Also, on Friday was the staff vs. student basketball game and pep rally. The last day was often the student's favorite day because they got to challenge the teachers and play basketball.

Jamal and Ellis chose not to attend so they could study real estate, and luckily, the librarian at the school had already been doing it for some years, so they were able to pick her brain any time of the day during school.

A dateless Ellis was ready to still attend the homecoming dance, but first, it was the homecoming football game. During halftime, the student body announced who won homecoming king and queen, which was the most convenient prize of them all. A confused Jamal and Ellis didn't know what to expect when they went to the game. All they knew was they were able to provide some type of balance between their social life and academic life. Both were equally necessary. Sabrina, Jamal's date to the dance, was hesitant to attend the game because she did not want Jamal to see her until he picked her up for the dance. As Jamal and Ellis continued enjoying the festivities of the game, they looked to their right and saw a student being bullied. The two boys quickly ran to that student's aid, and after doing so, they became instantly connected to that student whose name was Justin. Ellis and Justin's bond grew stronger and stronger over the next few weeks so much, so they began walking to school with one another, excluding Jamal.

Homecoming seemed to be a rite of passage for incoming freshmen. The reason being they got an opportunity to test their level of confidence when it came to the opposite sex. Ellis was content going without a date since the experience he had with asking out his crush did not go as he planned. Although Ellis did not have a date, he did not seem to care because he knew he would be able to attract girls once he arrived, and in fact, he was confident he would be able to make his crush Angelica jealous because, after all, she did hurt his feelings.

Jamal and Ellis left the game a little bit early, mainly so they could get back to Jamal's house to figure out their outfits and what they were going to wear. Jamal decided on blue slacks, a white button-up, and a blue tie that he did not know how to tie, so he asked his grandma, and luckily she knew how to tie it. Ellis wore black slacks, a white button-up, and a black tie.

Jamal felt the pressure of trying to make sure he matched his date Sabrina to a certain extent, so he called her and asked her, "Are we supposed to match one another?"

She replied, "Yea, I think so," and they both laughed.

Sabrina asked him what colors he was wearing, and after Jamal replied, she said, "Great, see you soon," and hung up the phone.

As Jamal and Ellis headed to the dance on foot, Ellis asked Jamal if he was alright with picking up Justin on the way. Jamal was hesitant at first but eventually agreed to do so. As they approached Justin's house, they noticed another teenage boy walking on the other side of the street, but they didn't pay much attention to it. Unlike Jamal and Ellis, Justin decided to wear jeans and a polo shirt because he said, "Wearing church clothes makes me uncomfortable."

As the three young men walked to the school for the dance, they all talked about how they were going to ask a girl to dance. Jamal said, "I think I won't need to ask because my date knows we are going to dance."

Ellis said, "I'm going to wait for a girl to ask me." Jamal and Justin both laughed and said, "Maaannnn, ain't no girl going to ask you to dance."

Meanwhile Justin, the one who seemed pretty confident, said, "I'm going to walk up to her and ask her to dance, keeping it nice and simple." Ellis and Jamal were confused and excited at the same time because he seemed so confident.

As they entered the dance, they were all so excited because neither one of them had ever experienced anything like that. Seeing their peers having fun by dancing, taking pictures, and making videos, I could go on and on. The boys were also able to see some of their teachers let their guards down, see them dance, see them laugh with their students, and all in all, it was an awesome experience.

As Jamal anxiously awaited the arrival of Sabrina, he saw another girl and decided to dance with her. Of course, as harmless as it was, he didn't understand how that would look as her friends saw him. Jamal was completely unaware of his surroundings and who was watching him. Sabrina finally arrived, and she was as beautiful as ever. Jamal couldn't take his eyes off of her as he walked toward the entrance and greeted her. He couldn't help but say, "Damn, Sabrina, you look good as hell."

Jamal was like a fish out of water in respect to how to navigate this new and exciting world he was in. Sabrina was so excited to be in his presence just as much as Jamal was excited to be in her presence. Jamal was trying to figure out a clever way to ask Sabrina if she wanted to dance but was nervous about doing so. Sabrina made up her mind after having talks with her mom about how to be on a date with a guy she liked. Her mom told her, "Make sure you try your best to empower him to want to be the best he can for you."

Sabrina asked, "How do I do that?"

Her mom replied, "Just have fun, Sabrina, don't overthink it. He likes you."

Jamal started to feel like he was under a lot of pressure because he saw most of his peers dancing and having a good time. Mind you, most of those peers were older than him, but he didn't see it that way. Although he felt all of that pressure, he did finally decide he would ask Sabrina to dance, and she happily said, "Yes."

This was both of their first times dancing with the opposite sex. Both Jamal and Sabrina were able to thoroughly enjoy one another and create a space where they both could develop and maintain a space of comfort for one another. After the dance, Jamal walked Sabrina home, and he wanted to be completely transparent and share some things with her that he had not even shared with his closest guy friends. He told Sabrina that his grandma had breast cancer and that she didn't have much longer to live.

Sabrina stopped walking, looked at Jamal and gave him a big hug, and told him, "I am here for you. I know that had to be hard to share with me, but I'm glad you trust me enough to tell me."

Jamal felt like a huge weight was lifted off of his shoulder, and now he could trust Sabrina even more. As Jamal was walking her to her house, he was trying to figure out how to ask for a kiss. As they were walking coincidentally, Sabrina was hoping Jamal would ask for one because she did not want to be the one to initiate it at all. Jamal told himself he would ask, and whatever happened after that, he would be fine with it, so he grabbed Sabrina's hand, pulled her close to him, and gave her a kiss. She accepted it and gave him a kiss as well. He told her to have a goodnight and that he would call her in the morning. As he walked back home, he couldn't help but be full of excitement and happiness. He took his crush on a date and got a kiss from her. Nothing could go wrong at this point, so he thought...

Chapter Three

J amal entered his house and saw his grandma passed out on the living room floor. He ran in and checked her pulse, tried calling her name several times, then he realized he needed to call 911, and he did just that.

"911, what's your emergency?"

"It's my grandma, she's lying on our living room floor, and she isn't breathing."

"How long has she been passed out?"

"I'm not sure. I just got back home from a school dance. Can someone hurry and get here quick?!"

"Of course, sir, I'm sending someone now. Try to remain calm".

"Alright, thanks!"

The ambulance finally arrived, good thing it only took them 10 minutes, but it seemed like forever to Jamal. Jamal's neighbor came over once she heard him yelling and screaming uncontrollably and did her best to calm him down by trying to reassure him that everything was going to be okay. For some reason, Jamal just did not feel the same. The ambulance took her to the nearest emergency room, about 15 minutes away from their house.

Once they arrived, they tried their best to revive her and were unsuccessful, Jamal was on his way to the hospital, and before getting there, he was overwhelmed with emotion and already had the feeling of his grandma transitioning. He also called Sabrina as he was on his way to the hospital and wanted to hear her voice. He was hesitant to let her know what was going on, but she was able to hear some nervousness in his voice, and he quickly said he was calling her back.

Sabrina grew more and more anxious as she waited on a call back from Jamal. Needless to say, he never returned her call. Jamal arrived at the hospital, and normally you would see and hear about people running to the front desk to figure out where the loved one was, but for some reason, Jamal did not run. As a matter of fact, he walked ever so calmly and asked the front desk clerk, "Which room is Rose Douglas in? She was just admitted less than 10 minutes ago."

The nurse replied, "Room 27, just right around this corner."

Jamal took one deep breath as he walked around the corner, preparing to hear the worst news to this point of his life.

The doctor stopped him before entering and asked him, "Are you Jamal?"

Jamal replied, "Yes, sir, is everything alright with my grandma?"

The doctor responded, "No, unfortunately, she didn't make it." Jamal asked the doctor if he could see her one last time. The doctor reluctantly replied and said, "Sure, young man."

Jamal and his neighbor walked into the room. He said he could feel the presence of his grandma instantly, so much so it scared him and made him feel a certain amount of emptiness. Jamal just wanted to lay with his grandma one last time, but unfortunately, he wasn't allowed to do so. However, he was able to give her one last kiss goodbye, and he whispered in her ear, "I'm going to make you proud, and I'm going to keep you in my heart."

The neighbor dropped Jamal back off at home after a long silent ride back home. The neighbor encouraged him to pack some clothes and stay with her until they were able to figure out Jamal's living situation. Jamal was so confused and felt defeated. Once Jamal arrived back home, he was faced with a dilemma, should he call Sabrina back or wait until the next day to talk to her so he could gather his thoughts and be able to speak to her clearly. He decided not to call her back that night, mainly because he was filled with emotion and didn't want her to hear or see him in that way. Jamal has a hard time falling asleep, as he was completely uncomfortable and learning how to adjust without his grandma being in the other room and hearing her snoring. It actually made him chuckle just thinking about her snoring and actually missing it.

*****

The next morning he didn't want to go to school because he didn't want to have to tell his friends that his grandmother had passed away. In fact, he tried to convince himself not to tell anyone. Not sure how he was going to manage to do that, but he definitely gave it some serious thought. He went to school the next morning, and he tried to be his normal self, but during his walk to school, he couldn't help but cry his eyes out, and he felt like he was able to have a full conversation with his grandma, he could vividly hear her say, "I love you my son, and you're going to do great things." He wanted to walk to Sabrina's house, so he did just that.

Before he could knock on the door, she opened the door and was so happy to see Jamal, but she did notice his energy was a bit off and wanted to know why. As they began walking to school, Jamal was thinking about how and when he would mention his grandma transitioning, so after about 10 minutes of walking, he finally decided to open up and talk to her about it. Jamal said, "I need to tell you something."

Sabrina responded, "What's up, Jamal? Is everything alright?"

"No, my grandma passed away over the weekend. She was passed out when I got back home from the homecoming dance. I was so scared and didn't know what to do. I screamed so loudly that my neighbor heard me and helped as much as she could."

Sabrina was speechless and didn't know exactly how to support, so she just stopped in her tracks, grabbed him, and hugged him as long and tight as she could. Jamal was so relieved, and as he hugged Sabrina, he couldn't help but be filled with so much emotion and cry as they were close to the school. Some of his schoolmates saw him and so stopped as they were walking. Some asked their parents to pull over. Once he saw how much love and support he was receiving, he immediately became grateful and appreciative, and those feelings of embarrassment quickly became non-existent.

Although a lot of his peers knew what had happened, his best friend Ellis was still unaware. In fact, he arrived at school late that day because he had to take care of his mom and was starting to realize her time was coming to an end, so once they saw each other, they both seemed exhausted from the weekend, and Jamal told Ellis he had something to tell him. "My grandma passed away over the weekend. She was passed out on the living room floor once I got back home from the dance."

Ellis looked at Jamal and said, "I'm here for you, bro, you're my best friend, and I'm with you until the end."

Now Ellis faced a dilemma on whether he would tell Jamal

about his tough weekend or not, and he decided to wait and not say anything, mainly because he just didn't know how after receiving the information Jamal gave him. So the three continued to walk to school as if nothing had been told. Jamal wanted to make it very clear that he didn't want anyone else to know who already knows, mainly because he didn't want pity or people pretending to care about him and how he felt.

Chapter Four

Sabrina also was dealing with some issues of her own. Her dad was now trying to re-enter her life after fourteen years of being completely absent and non-existent. Her mom was indifferent about the situation and really wanted to support Sabrina with this situation but also introduced the idea of therapy for them both. Her mom asked her to research therapy and let her know how she felt about possibly receiving it. She expected her to have an answer within the next few days. After days of researching and understanding the concept of therapy, Sabrina decided to go with her mom. Sabrina didn't think anything of it in regard to her and her mom going, but she would soon find out some things about her mom's past she had no idea about.

On their way to the therapist, Sabrina's mom wanted to fill her in a little bit about what she was going to say so that it wouldn't come as a complete shock. Her mom said, "Sabrina, when I was a child, about eight or nine years old, my mom beat me really badly because I lost something that was very valuable to her. Since then, her and my relationship has been extremely rocky, which is why you have never met her."

Sabrina sat and listened and was confused but did not want to make it about her. She told her mom she loved her and that she had her back one hundred percent. They walked into the office, and they instantly loved the energy they felt. Dr. Sharice Shepard was really excited to get to know these women and was filled with joy that it was a black mom and daughter seeking out therapy because it wa something that didn't happen as often as it probably should.

As the three women began to talk and introduced themselves, Sabrina was filled with nervousness and wasn't fully sure how to navigate in that space, simply because she was in a space where two grown women who had fully matured were beginning to engage in conversation about their childhood that she personally couldn't relate to just yet. Dr. Sharice asked her mom to start from the beginning of her childhood from what she could remember, and fortunately or unfortunately, her memory was not in question at all.

She began to tell her about how she didn't feel like her dad loved her at all, mainly because he would never tell her he loved her or hug her or show any type of affection toward her. Dr. Sharice was so proud of her mom for sharing that information. In fact, she wished her, and her mom would've gone through therapy as well to repair their broken relationship. Dealing with trauma is and will always be a real thing for most people if not all. Sabrina was learning new words and learning new things about her mom and was beginning to understand that her mom was and still is a scarred woman. Dr. Sharice asked Sabrina if she knew what the definition of trauma was, and Sabrina did not know, so she gave Sabrina the definition, which was "a deeply distressing or disturbing experience."

"Trauma in our community is often suppressed because it is easier to do so. Instead of addressing it or trying to address it, the best way for me to address my trauma was to go to the source, and I realized that source was my mom and dad. Unfortunately, everyone isn't able to still have both parents alive in order to be able to do so, but if you are still afforded that luxury, I strongly recommend having those difficult conversations," stated Dr. Sharice.

Sabrina's mom was in awe of how much Dr. Sharice was personally willing to share. Her initial impression of the therapist was that they just wanted to hear about their client's experiences and were not really willing to share their own, but she was pleasantly surprised to find out that wasn't the case. Sabrina was curious to hear what her mom had to say about her childhood experience. A lot of things happened to her that she knew about but didn't know full details of because she didn't know how to inquire about those details.

Dr. Sharice asked her to share her most memorable experience as a child, good or bad. Her mom said she would talk about a good experience as well as share a bad experience to provide balance to the conversation. As she started to talk, her eyes began to water, and she became overwhelmed with emotion as she struggled to speak clearly without crying. Sabrina did not know how to support her mom because she had never seen her that way at all. Sabrina went to grab her mom's hand. When she did so, her mom grabbed it and felt more comfortable knowing her daughter was there to fully support her, as this was not easy for her at all.

Dr. Sharice said, "Take as much time as you need."

Her mom replied, "I'm ready to share this experience. This is the first time I've actually thought about it in a long time. When I was nine years old, I was bullied by a girl named Michelle Nixon. She bullied me so bad I wouldn't want to go to school, I wouldn't want to eat, she was so mean to me and my friends, and we didn't understand or know why."

That conversation then triggered Dr. Sharice to ask Sabrina if she had ever experienced any bullying or mistreatment from her peers. Sabrina couldn't recall, which was a good sign of her not experiencing any bullying to this point. Her mom was glad and gave her a big hug and whispered in her ear, saying, "I love you, daughter." Sabrina being the only child was left to sit and wonder how she could support her mom once they left Dr. Sharice's office. Sabrina's mom also wanted to share her most positive experience as a child, which was, going fishing with her dad. She loved waking up every Saturday morning and spending that quality time with him. She recalled catching four fish, which was extremely hard to do, as she said. Sabrina saw her face light up with joy and wanted to take a picture to capture that moment, and she did just that.

Their first therapy session was a huge success because her mom opened up and was able to free herself from some of her past trauma. Healing from anything takes time, and you have to be very intentional about it. A lot of times, we just need an outlet and don't know how to go about finding that outlet, but therapy did it for her mom, and it can work for you too. The car ride home was awkward for the first ten to fifteen minutes, but at that point, both mom and daughter looked at one another at a stop light and began laughing and crying tears of joy.

*****

Once they arrived back home, Sabrina eagerly wanted to call Jamal and let her know what she had just experienced. She also wanted to bring some joy to his life as well as best she could. But before she called Jamal, she wanted to have a follow-up conversation with her mom and ask her, "Did she ever see the woman again that was bullying her?"

Her mom replied, "No, I have not, but if I did, it would be no hard feelings because I know she was just mimicking behavior she saw from someone else and that she didn't know any better."

Sabrina was excited to ask her that question, along with when the next time they will be seeing Dr. Sharice, and mom replied, "In two weeks." All Sabrina could do was smile and say, "Alright, mom, I can't wait."

After that short but much-needed conversation with her mom, she called Jamal and wanted to express to him what she and her mom had just experienced to talk through her childhood traumas. Jamal had never heard that word before and wanted her to explain what it meant. Jamal was really fixated on that word and wanted to explore it more. He then began to ask himself if he dealt with any trauma and, if so, how he handled it. 9th graders being introduced to trauma, what it meant, and how it was manifested was truly an amazing thing.

Jamal was very curious about Sabrina's therapy session and began to ask several questions about it, but before Sabrina could answer any of his questions, Jamal began to think to himself that it might be a great idea for him to look into receiving therapy. Sabrina continued the conversation with Jamal and said, "I'm so proud of my mom and what she had to endure, and I'm glad bullying hasn't affected me or even happened to me."

Jamal asked Sabrina, "Do you think your mom would be cool with me going with you guys the next time?"

Sabrina replied and said, "I think that's a great idea, and I will ask her; I'm going to go ask her right now. Hold on!"

Jamal paced back and forth, nervous about what her saying, yes or no. He started to regret asking Sabrina that because he didn't want to ruin the good relationship he and her mother had. About ten minutes later, Sabrina finally came back to the phone. Luckily, Sabrina came back and said, "My mom would love for you to join us."

Jamal yelled with excitement and extreme gratitude for Sabrina and her mom. He asked Sabrina if he could thank her mom, Sabrina said, "Hold on, let me go get her."

"Hi, Jamal. Sabrina and I would be honored for you to join us in a couple of weeks to visit Ms. Sharice Shepard. She is really amazing."

Jamal said, "Thank you so much. I look forward to sharing this wonderful experience with you all, Sabrina has introduced something new to me, and I love it."

As soon as he got off the phone with Sabrina and her mom, he began writing in his journal, writing about going to visit and therapist and how nervous and excited he was, and how he couldn't wait to be able to talk to someone about everything he was experiencing and everything he had experienced with his grandma passing away. Also, how he was staying with his god mom, who was also his neighbor. He was so grateful for her and the sacrifices she had made for him. Jamal wrote in his journal about how much he loved real estate and how he wanted to get involved with it after high school or even before he graduated from high school. Despite knowing how intelligent academically he was, he really had no intentions of going to college because he saw it as being very expensive and just not worth it in the long run, based on stories he had heard from older people in his life. He had realized that writing in his journal was helping him cope with a lot of his feelings and calming him down tremendously, so much so that he committed to writing something in his journal every day. He had not told anyone about it, but one of his teachers spoke to him about journaling, and he had been hooked ever since.

Chapter Five

The next morning, he went to pick up Ellis so they could walk to school. At that point, he wanted to talk to him about his journaling and going to see a therapist with Sabrina and was excited to tell him about both new things in his life. But before he could mention any of it, he saw how tired and just drained Ellis looked, so he asked him, "Is everything all right, bro?"

Ellis said, "Yea, I'm good, bro."

The two continued to walk, and Jamal stopped and said, "Naw, bro, something is not right. Talk to me. I am here for you."

Ellis looked at him and said, "I'm scared, bro. I don't want my mom to die," as tears began to form in both of his eyes.

Jamal said, "I can only imagine how scared you must be, and I empathize with you, bro. I really do, but you aren't alone, and I will always have your back."

Ellis needed to hear that from his best friend and was glad he did. The level of vulnerability both young men were able to share was simply amazing and truly inspiring. The two arrived at school feeling much better about everything they discussed with one another. Jamal met up with Sabrina and gave her the biggest hug, and wanted to thank her in person for the amount of support she had provided to him.

As ninth graders, both Jamal and Sabrina were much more mature than most their age. Their experiences had helped them reach that level. For Jamal, not really having a relationship with his parents and then losing his grandmother can cause a teen to do two things, either self-destruct or stay encouraged and continue to strive for greatness, which he decided to do the ladder. Sabrina had a different story, but it ultimately led her to that same maturity stage as Jamal. Sabrina had never met her dad, and although she wanted to ask her mom about him, she struggled with doing so. She remembered receiving a birthday card from him when she turned five, but that was the last contact she had had with him. Jamal knew and understood he was having a hard time coping with his grandmother's transitioning, but he hoped that going to therapy with Sabrina and her mom would help.

Jamal came back home and let his godmother know that he would be going to therapy with Sabrina and her mom tomorrow afternoon. She asked him if he was nervous or afraid and if he had a good understanding of what therapy was. Jamal responded and said, "I sure do. Sabrina did a great job of explaining what it is and also talking about her experience when she went with her mom last week."

Jamal's godmother responded with a smile and said, "I am very proud of you, my son, and your grandmother is proud of you as well." Jamal went to sleep feeling great about going to the therapist the next morning with Sabrina and her mom, so much so he was unable to sleep because he was filled with excitement.

*****

The next morning, Sabrina called Jamal at 7:20 AM to give him a wake-up call, but that wasn't necessary because Jamal had already been up since 6:00 AM. Their appointment was at 8:30, and they did not want to be even one minute late. Sabrina and her mom told Jamal they would be leaving their house at 7:45 AM so they could beat any traffic that may slow them down. They arrived to pick up Jamal at 8:10 and had 20 minutes to get to the session, which was more than enough time because there was hardly any traffic.

Once they arrived at Dr. Sharice's office, Jamal suddenly became nervous, knees weak, and for some reason, his heart was beating really fast. He had been looking forward to this day but also was unaware of what to expect and if he would be able to handle what was to come. He decided to wait in the car to relax and come to full grips with what was on the horizon, he also began to think about Sabrina and her mom being there and if he actually wanted to open up and be vulnerable with them being present. He did feel great because it was a sunny day, with not a cloud in the sky, the sun just shining.

He said to himself in the car, "You can do this, you will do this, you have the strength and the courage."

He learned to speak life into himself from his grandmother. She would often say uplifting and encouraging words to herself, such as, "You can do this, and I love you." She would always tell herself she loved herself, and Jamal used to think it was weird, but once she passed, he began to see the true benefit of being able to speak life into yourself regardless of the situation or circumstance.

Jamal mustered up the strength to get out of the car and make his way into Dr. Sharice's office, but he wanted Sabrina to meet him at the door and walk him in. He was then greeted with the biggest hug and embrace from Dr. Sharice. She also whispered in his ear, "I admire you and your strength. My condolences about your grandma."

Dr. Sharice asked Sabrina's mom if it was alright to speak to Jamal and have him introduce himself.

Sabrina's mom responded, "Of course." This was the moment

Jamal had been waiting for, he now had the space to be fully vulnerable and transparent about how he felt about everything, and when I say everything, I mean everything.

Dr. Sharice asked him, "What do you remember about your biological parents? It can be positive or negative, don't feel like you have to only remember great things because the reality of it is that is not always the reality."

Jamal dropped his head and left it down for at least 30 seconds, came back up, and said, "I truly don't remember much negative or positive. Is there a way I can remember, or was I just too young to remember?"

Dr. Sharice said, "Well, it all depends, it could be that you were too young, or it could mean that you've suppressed those memories, and when we suppress things, sometimes it makes it hard for us to relive them."

Jamal said, "What does suppress mean?"

Dr. Sharice said, "I am going to give you the same definition google has, which is, prevent the development, action, or expression of (a feeling, impulse, idea, etc.); restrain, in some instances, it is good to suppress things, and in other instances, it may not be, but it all depends on the individual, and neither one is deemed as right or wrong. Based on that response and definition, do you think you have suppressed those feelings, or do you need more time to give that some thought?" Dr. Sharice asked Jamal.

Jamal said, "Wow, I am definitely going to need more time to think about that."

Unlike most therapists, Dr. Sharice was the type of person that liked to develop a strong bond and relationship with her clients, so much so that she also liked to discuss her past traumas and loved to show how vulnerable she was so that her clients felt comfortable to do so as well. So she made the conscious decision to open up to Jamal about her past experiences with close friends and family members passing away but specifically her grandma on her mom's side. She was able to empathize with Jamal and truly understand the pain he was going through from losing his grandma, especially because she was his sole provider and caretaker.

Dr. Sharice asked Jamal, "What do you think is the best lesson your grandma told you or you taught her?" Jamal was surprised that she asked, *'what was the best lesson you taught her?'* he actually was stuck on that question and wanted to think back to anything that he may have taught her directly or indirectly.

Sabrina and her mom anxiously sat in on Jamal's session and immediately became overwhelmed with emotion, and they both were unable to hold back their tears. Jamal explained in great detail the relationship with his grandma and how he wished he had that same relationship with his mom. Dr. Sharice asked him if he would want to meet his mom. Jamal replied back and said, "I honestly don't know, a part of me wants to, and then the other part of me wouldn't know how to have a conversation with her."

Sabrina listened in and couldn't imagine what it would be like to have never met her mom since she and her mom had such a great relationship. Although Jamal had never met her, he still had so much love and respect for her, which Sabrina and her mom appreciated a lot. Jamal had never spoken badly about her, which was surprising on so many different levels. He often said he would rather focus on having positive thoughts about her versus having negative ones. In fact, his grandma really helped him understand that concept because even when he would have negative thoughts about her, he would always communicate them to his grandma, and she would always encourage him to channel his thoughts and energy differently when it came to his mom.

Dr. Sharice asked Jamal, "Do you know anything about your dad?"

Jamal responded and said, "I don't know anything at all. My grandma told me where he lived before and drove me by his house, and she asked me if I wanted to get out and go see him, but I didn't know what to expect, so I decided to avoid that situation altogether."

While all of this is being said, both Sabrina and her mom were right there supporting Jamal and doing so by holding his hand and rubbing his back for comfort. Dr. Sharice encouraged Sabrina and her mom to continue to support him in his journey, and they both agreed to do so.

Jamal thanked Dr. Sharice for her insight and let her know he did not take it for granted and was looking forward to reflecting on their conversation once he left and made it back home. Sabrina's mom was ready to pick up from their conversation from last week. She asked Dr. Sharice, "What do you recommend for me to do in regard to having these kinds of conversations with my daughter? I want her to know certain things, but I also don't want to overwhelm her."

Dr. Sharice said, "It will really help your relationship with your daughter, but also having that level of vulnerability will also free yourself from harboring so much hurt and pain from your past. Also, it can and will help Sabrina with learning how to communicate certain feelings and emotions as she continues to mature and grow into her womanhood." Dr. Sharice asked Sabrina, "Would you like for your mom to talk to you more about her past?"

Sabrina said, "Yes, I would love that." Sabrina was excited to hear more about her mom's upbringing, and how she became the woman she is, Sabrina looks up to her mom so much and really values and appreciates her. Sabrina's mom wanted to reflect on the relationship or lack thereof with her dad, but before she was able to actually speak on it, she was overwhelmed with emotion just thinking about their relationship and how it became non-existent as she got older. She acknowledged that the men she would begin to have an interest in were the main reason for their relationship to dissolve.

She could recall an incident that occurred when she was in the eleventh grade between her boyfriend at the time and her dad. They got into a heated argument because Sabrina's mom tried to sneak out of their house to go with him to see a movie, and her dad caught her. Once he caught her, he said, "Where do you think you are going with that boy?"

She replied and said, "I'd rather be where he is than at home with you," to her dad.

From that moment on, their relationship was never the same. Her dad was unable to express to his daughter that she hurt his feelings and instead decided to distance himself from her. Dr. Sharice asked her, "Would you have done anything differently with that situation?"

She replied and said, "Of course." If he was here now, what would you say to him? She takes one look at Sabrina with tears in her eyes and says, "This is something I've thought about and asked myself hundreds of times, probably thousands of times at this point, but I thank you so much for asking me that and holding me accountable for

truly giving thought into answering the question." Here goes nothing",
Sabrina's mom says. "First of all, I want to apologize to you, dad. I
was wrong for choosing a boyfriend over you. I miss you so much. I
miss the bond we used to have. I miss the conversations we used to
have. All in all, I miss us. I've spent the majority of my life wondering
how you were doing, wondering if you were missing me as much as I
miss you. I often replay that day in my head, and I can never
understand why I chose to react the way I did. I didn't think they
would ruin our relationship because I wanted to do what I wanted and
didn't expect that to cause as much pain as it did to you. I hope you
find it in your heart to forgive me so we can go back to the relationship
we used to have. I do have one question because I have always
wondered how that interaction made you feel? Did you feel like I
chose him over you? And is there anything you would do differently?"

Sabrina looked at her mom as tears began to fall down her face,
and she said, "I am so proud of you mom, I know that was not easy
for you to do."

Chapter Six

The following Monday at school, Jamal spent a lot of time by himself, mainly to reflect on that visit with Dr. Sharice. For some reason, he felt more comfortable being alone. As he was walking to his fourth-period class after lunch, he ran into Ellis, not that he was trying to avoid him, but he didn't expect to bump into him. Jamal was very short with Ellis, saying, "What's up? I'll talk to you later. I'm headed to my math class."

With their ninth-grade year quickly coming to an end, Ellis couldn't help but think their friendship was taking a turn for the worst. Ellis was able to maintain a 3.7 GPA throughout the year, and Jamal was able to maintain a 4.0 GPA. Sabrina maintained a 3.5 GPA. Ellis left school early that day because he was called to the office for an emergency; not sure what happened, Ellis quickly rushed to the office, and when he got there, he was greeted by his auntie and his uncle, letting him know his mom had passed away due to a heart attack. Ellis couldn't do anything but look at his aunt and uncle, and before he could ask any questions, he dropped to the ground and began crying uncontrollably.

All four students know the importance of getting their education, and all have committed to doing just that. Although Jamal and Ellis have aspirations of building their own real estate company, they also put a tremendous amount of value into taking full advantage of their schooling. Their ninth-grade year has been full of ups and downs, but all in all, they loved their first year of high school and are looking forward to their next three years in high school.

During that summer, Jamal and Ellis spent just about every single day together. They wanted to start brainstorming ideas about their before-mentioned real estate company; not having much knowledge about it, they set out to research as much about it as possible. While researching, they realized more and more how possible this dream was. However, they didn't realize what type of sacrifices they would have to make in order to continue to manifest what they knew was possible.

For example, Jamal would end up spending less time with Sabrina, and she would begin to grow weary and confused as to why Jamal and Ellis decided to not tell anyone about what they had been doing because they didn't want any outside entities discouraging them. Once Sabrina found out what was going on, she wasn't mad or upset. In fact, she wanted to help them as best she could. She began to learn more and more about ownership and began to understand the importance of it. So much so that she even spoke to her mom about it.

Her mom said to her, "Ownership is what you should strive for, ownership is what I want for you, ownership is what you should want for yourself."

So, Sabrina took that to heart. Sabrina was finally going to get a chance to talk to Dr. Sharice and relished the opportunity to do so. She wanted to talk to her about ownership and the relationship with her father or lack thereof. She has been wanting to talk to her mom about that more and more but hasn't quite figured out the best way to do so; even though her mom has never talked negatively about him, she still feels like there might still be a soft spot for her mom and doesn't want to reopen old wounds so to speak.

Upon entering Dr. Sharice's office, she asked her mom if she could speak to her privately; she felt much more comfortable doing so. The first thing Sabrina said was, "I don't want to waste any time. How do I tell my mom I want a relationship with my dad?"

Dr. Sharice's response was, "Talk to me about the current relationship you have with him, if any."

"I don't have a relationship with him at all."

Dr. Sharice asks, "Why didn't you want your mom in here for this conversation?"

Sabrina said, "Because I didn't want to say anything that would possibly hurt her feelings, we rarely discuss my dad at all, and when we do, it's mainly general conversation, nothing too specific."

"What are your thoughts on me bringing your mom in, and we all have this conversation together?"

She still expressed how uncomfortable she was doing so by saying, "Not just yet. I still want to fully be confident in being able to express my feelings to her, and right now, I'm not confident in being able to."

Dr. Sharice says, "The only way to be fully comfortable is to do it, say what is on your mind, trust your thoughts and feelings."

Sabrina's mom anxiously waits in the waiting room and can't help but wonder and think about what her daughter is saying and how she is feeling to not want her to be present in the room with them. Although she is slightly confused, she's more concerned about Sabrina and her emotional well-being. She remembered them talking in the car on the way to the office, and Sabrina said she was nervous about today's session and didn't know what the outcome would be, and now her mom understands why. She began reading old text messages from her and Sabrina, and she began crying because of how close and loving they were to one another.

Dr. Sharice then comes out to get her from the waiting room, she says, "Sabrina would like to say some things to you, but before she does, I want to encourage you to be fully present and not take anything she says personally."

Her mom responds and says, "Will do!"

Before Sabrina can say anything, she holds her mom's hand and then takes a deep breath, "Mom, I love you with all of my heart. I appreciate everything we have been through. I also appreciate you opening up the way you did a few weeks ago. The reason why I wanted to talk to Dr. Sharice alone was that I was scared, scared to tell you how I felt about my dad. I want/need a relationship with him. Are you mad at him for leaving us?"

Her mom looks at her as tears begin to form in both of her eyes and says, "I apologize for thinking you didn't need him. I also apologize for thinking I could raise you all by myself, and I knew then how selfish that was, and I know now how selfish that is and just like you, I was scared. I recognize that the way I have handled this situation has not been the best but baby girl, I've always wanted the best for you despite the mistakes I have made in the process."

Sabrina needed to hear that from her mom. She was excited to hear her mom take full responsibility for her wrongdoings, mainly because she heard her mom say a lot, "Take responsibility for your actions no matter how tough it is." Sabrina was happy to hear her mom practice what she preached. Sabrina then asked her mom, "Can we call my dad once we leave her so I can talk to him because I need to ask him some questions as well and hold him accountable? I am so thankful for you teaching me how to do so by watching you and listening to how you communicate with your friends and loved ones."

Her mom responds and says, "Of course, we can call him. As a matter of fact, I will give you his phone number right now."

Dr. Sharice tells Sabrina that she is proud of her and respects the way she chose to approach this situation. Sabrina was filled with joy and couldn't wait to call Jamal and tell him what just happened and how understanding her mom was. That truly instilled a different level of confidence in Sabrina.

*****

Jamal was hanging out with Ellis when he received a call from Sabrina. Eager to talk to her, he told Ellis he was going to step outside. For some strange reason, he knew their conversation was going to be a good one. Their conversation was not just a good one but a great one.

"Jamal says, "What's up, Sabrina? How was your session?"

Sabrina responds and says, "It was great, Jamal, like really great. I was finally able to talk to my mom about my dad and wanting to have a relationship with him. As you know, I was so nervous to do so, but once I began talking, it became easier and easier to express my feelings. I want to give my mom a real shout-out too because she was so intentional about listening to me and really wanted to help me."

Jamal says, "Wow, I am so proud of both of you! That is so inspiring. What's next in regard to building that relationship with your dad?"

Sabrina says, "I have his phone number, and I am going to give him a call because I need to ask him some very important questions."

Jamal asks, "What do you want to ask him?" Sabrina says, "I really need to know why he hasn't been there, but I am scared to ask because I don't know what his response is going to be, but I can't focus on that."

*****

Later that evening, Sabrina decided to give her dad a call. It was about 8:20 PM pacific standard time. Unsure where he lived, and if that would be too late for him, she decided to call anyway because she didn't want to waste any more time. She called, and the phone rang two times, then her dad answered the phone, "Hello, this is Keith. Who is calling?"

Sabrina responds and says, "This is Sabrina, your fourteen-year-old daughter." She also hears what sounds like an infant in the background crying.

He says, "Sabrina? My baby girl Sabrina?"

She replies and says, "Yes, dad, it is me! I miss you so much. I think about you all of the time."

Keith, who is filled with joy and excitement, says, "My baby girl, I miss you too. I can't believe this," as he laughs. "How are you? Where are you? How's school going? How's your mom doing?"

Sabrina is so happy that her dad is happy to hear from her. She says, "Jeez, dad, that's a lot of questions," as she laughs. "I've been wanting to call you. I've been needing to call you. Why haven't you called me or reached out to me?"

Her dad responds and says, "I've also been wanting to do the same, and I'm not going to make any excuses as to why I didn't. I want to take full responsibility for not being a father to you, you didn't deserve that, and you don't deserve that at all. I'm so proud of you, and I'm also proud of your mom for raising such an amazing young woman."

Sabrina says, "Thanks, Dad. I really appreciate you for acknowledging my mom's greatness and also for taking full responsibility for your absence."

Keith says, "Of course! I'm looking forward to us working on our relationship and picking up where we left off if that is alright with you?"

Sabrina says, "Yes, dad! I would love that! I can't wait to talk to my mom about our conversation. She's going to be so happy for us! She and I have been going to see a therapist about a lot of different things she and I struggle with, and I spoke to our therapist about missing you and wanting to talk to you about not being there for me. How that really has affected me because I truly didn't understand why. I still have more questions to ask you, but I will wait to do that in person."

Keith says, "I completely understand all the concerns you have/had, and I want to be able to answer and respond to them all because I was wrong, and you didn't deserve me not being there for you and to answer your first question, you didn't do anything wrong at all! With that being said, I want to apologize to you, and I also want to say that moving forward, you will not have to worry about why I left because that will not happen again."

Sabrina accepts his apology and says, "I will talk to you later, dad. I'm going to talk to my mom about our conversation, and thank you again."

Keith says, "Sounds good, Sabrina. I love you, and tell your mom thank you for me. As a matter of fact, I will tell her myself. When do you think it is a good time to call your mom? Should I call now or wait until tomorrow afternoon?"

Sabrina says, "You should wait until tomorrow afternoon, she may need some time to talk to you, but I will let her know you want to talk to her. I don't think she will decline it, but you never know."

Keith says, "No problem. I completely understand. Talk to you later, Sabrina."

Sabrina was so excited about that conversation she couldn't wait to tell her mom about it, running to her mom's room and screaming her name, "Mom, mom, I just talked to my dad, and the conversation was so great! I wish you could've heard it. He took full responsibility for his actions in regards to not being around, he apologized to me, he told me he loved me and missed me, he also said he loves you and appreciates you for raising me and how he knows how difficult that had to have been. All in all, mom, I'm so glad I got a chance to talk to him. Lastly, he also wants to talk to you. He didn't say about what, but he did say he wanted to talk to you."

Sabrina's mom is excited that her daughter is excited and also wants to share that same excitement with her. She says, "I'm glad you talked to him. I'm glad he took responsibility for his actions. I would love to have a conversation with him. I think it is long overdue, he has always been a man I respected despite his lack of effort in being a father to you, but I will definitely hold him accountable for his lack of effort. I don't think I had ever talked to you about when he and I broke up. Although it wasn't a bad break-up, it was tough for both he and I, I'm not saying that to make an excuse for him, but I am saying that because I do and will always want to acknowledge his feelings as I am sure he will do mine. Your dad wanted to move to a different state, and I did not want to move at all. He wanted to move for a better job opportunity, and I thought he was being selfish because the way I interpreted it was, he wasn't asking me but more so telling me. So, about a month or two after that initial conversation about moving, he asked me why I didn't want to move, and I told him because my job is here, and so is my family. I believe that was the beginning of our downfall. I say downfall because from what I remember from that point on, it seemed as if everything was an argument, each of us wanting to prove to the other we were right instead of communicating effectively."

Sabrina says, "I can see how that could cause a division between you two. Do you think you guys could've worked it out? And did you guys try to?"

Sabrina's mom replies and says, "It definitely caused division between us both, so much so we would have a hard time having a general conversation without an argument eventually happening. As far as you asking me if we could've worked it out, I wasn't in the right state of mind to be able to do so, but if I could do it all over again, I would've worked it out. He was truly my best friend." Sabrina nods her head and then gives her mom a hug. Her mom then looks at her and thanks to her for being a good daughter.

Chapter Seven

The next day, Sabrina calls Jamal and tells him everything, from the conversation with her dad to the conversation with her mom after she talked to her dad. Jamal then says to her, "I'm ready to hear about all of it! Where do you want to start?"

Sabrina says, "First I called my dad, and of course I was nervous, but I did not let my nerves get the best of me. I told him how I felt. I told him I missed him and how much I loved him. He then apologized for being an absent father and took full responsibility for his actions. Then he said he wanted to talk to my mom, which kind of surprised me, but I'm glad he wanted to talk to her. All in all, I am so happy with how the conversation went, and I couldn't ask for a better outcome."

All Jamal could do was tell her how proud he was of her and how happy he was for her and her family. He then followed that up by saying, "I could only imagine how tough that was for you, and I'm glad you didn't let that stop you from achieving your goal."

Sabrina then said, "It's still so much to tell you, but I will wait to tell you everything else in person. When is the next time I'm going to see you?"

Jamal says, "I look forward to hearing everything else, and I'm free tomorrow after school. Does that work for you?"

Sabrina says, "Yes, tomorrow after school is perfect."

Jamal says, "Sounds good, I will see you tomorrow."

*****

Later that evening, at about 5 PM, Sabrina walks into her mom's room to remind her to give her dad a call. Much to her surprise, her mom had already spoken to Keith. Sabrina's mom says, "Well, my daughter, you are too late," as she said sarcastically. "We had such a great talk! As a matter of fact, we talked for about two hours, almost three."

Sabrina could do nothing but smile and jump up and down because she was so happy and excited. Sabrina says, "Mom, how did it go? Tell me everything I need to know."

Then she follows that by laughing out loud. Both Sabrina and her mom are so happy that neither can contain it nor do they want to. Both women were excited about different reasons. Sabrina is excited because she will finally be able to enjoy her dad in a way she has never been able to enjoy before. Sabrina's mom was happy because her daughter was happy and also because Keith apologized for his lack of maturity as well as for being absent in their daughters' life.

Sabrina now feels like she has her family back together, and all it took was some encouragement from Dr. Sharice, having the confidence to tell her mom what she was missing and what she needed, and her mom as well for instilling that confidence in her to be a confident young woman. Sabrina still had one more person to tell about her good news, and that was Dr. Sharice. For some reason, she was nervous to tell her, not because she was scared or afraid but more so because she was so appreciative and grateful for her for not only listening to her but providing a safe space for her to speak her truth. In fact, she wanted to speak to Dr. Sharice in person instead of telling her on the phone, and her mom fully supported that idea.

They were coming up on their last few sessions, and both women felt so empowered. Although Sabrina's mom was apprehensive to receive therapy, she is glad she made the decision to go through with it. She still has some things she would like to talk to Dr. Sharice about, but she feels confident that she will be able to get the closure she needs from those situations. She wants to go to her office by herself because she feels like she would be able to be fully transparent without her daughter present. She asked herself if she should feel that way about her not feeling comfortable without her daughter being present, and she convinced herself that Sabrina would understand.

Sabrina both excited and eager to see Dr. Sharice, asked her mom if they could change the days they go see her. Instead of Wednesday, could they go on Monday or Tuesday? Sabrina's mom replied and said, "I will reach out to Dr. Sharice and see, but I do want to talk to you about me going to see her alone. What are your thoughts about that?"

Sabrina replied and said, "No worries, mom, you have my full support to do so. You supported me when I wanted to talk to her alone."

Sabrina kept reliving that conversation with her dad, and by doing so, it inspired her to want to talk to him again, but now she was hoping to get that same level of interest from her dad. She was looking forward to him calling. Keith was at home and looking forward to calling his daughter because he knew how that would make her feel, and he wanted to bring her that same level of joy. So after work, he gave her a call, "Hello, Sabrina, this is your dad. How are you doing?!"

Sabrina says, "Dad, I was just thinking about you! I'm doing great, thanks for asking. How are you doing?"

Keith says, "I'm going good as well. I wanted to hear your voice and let you know I was thinking about you. I was telling your mom I currently live in Seattle, but I'm going to come to visit you within the next couple of weeks if that's alright with you".

Sabrina says, "Yes, that would be great! I'm looking forward to spending some time with you!"

Keith responds and says, "I am looking forward to spending time with you as well!"

Sabrina says, "Can I ask you a question, dad? Do you have any other children or a wife?"

Keith says, "I have two other daughters, and no, I am not married. My other two children are by the same woman, though. So, you have two sisters, and you're the oldest."

Sabrina is surprised and happy at the same time! She then says, "What are their names?!"

Keith says, "Imani and Cherish they're identical twins, but they're so different from one another it's pretty cool. I can't wait for you to meet them, and I know they feel the same way about wanting to meet them. They know about you and have often asked about you."

Sabrina says, "Wow! I have twin sisters?! How cool is that! Do they live with you? And how old are they?"

Keith answers and says, "You definitely have twin sisters. No, they don't live with me; they live with their mother not too far from where I live. They just turned eight years old. We threw them a small birthday party at her mom's house with some of their closest friends from school. They had a really good time."

Sabrina asks, "What's their mom's name?"

Keith says, "Nadine Wilkins. I met her about ten years ago. We used to work for the same Real Estate Agency here in Seattle, Washington."

Sabrina asks, "Do you still work for that same company? If so, do you enjoy it, or would you rather be doing something else?"

Keith says, "No, I don't work for that agency anymore, but I still work in real estate, it is my passion, and I love it."

Sabrina says, "Wow, dad! My boyfriend is also really into real estate, and I know you would like him a lot!"

Keith says, "You have a boyfriend? I would love to meet him; I know he must be a great guy if you like him, and it seems like you do just based on you mentioning him and telling me about him."

Sabrina says, "Yes, dad, I have a boyfriend," as she laughs out loud. "My mom likes him a lot, he is very respectful and encouraging, but I'll let you be the judge for yourself when you meet him."

Keith says, "Sounds good to me, I can come to visit you, or you can come to visit me. Which one do you prefer?"

Sabrina says, "I could easily come in the summer, but during the school year, it would be easier if you came to visit me out here in LA."

Keith says, "Good point. I will give your mom a call and talk to her about working out the logistics. I want to get down there within the next week, we have a lot of catching up to do, and I don't want to waste any more time."

Sabrina says, "I couldn't have said that better myself. This all seems so surreal, and I am just so happy for us and can't wait to build a relationship with you and my other sisters and with their mother."

Sabrina tells her mom about the conversation with her dad and lets her know her dad wants to come visit them within the next couple of weeks and her mom is equally excited. Her mom says, "I will call him so he and I can work out the details. The last time you saw your dad was when you were two years old, which I don't think you remember, but that was the last time I saw him as well." Sabrina yells and says, "I have to call Jamal. I can't wait another minute!

*****

Jamal is looking forward to hearing from Sabrina about her second conversation with her dad. As he is waiting for that call from her, he receives a call from Ellis and Ellis lets him know he may have to move to Houston, TX. Surprised by that, Jamal couldn't do anything but try to understand why. Ellis, on the other hand, was not offering up much information as to why. The reason for that was because he was confused and unsure how to communicate what happened with his dad's side of the family in Houston.

Ellis has visited his father a few times over the years, and he's always wanted to spend more time with him but wasn't able to do so. Ellis finds out he could be moving out there within the next month or so, maybe sooner. Jamal wants to be able to support his good friend but is not sure how to do so, mainly because he doesn't know if Ellis is being forced to move or if Ellis wants to move. Either way, Jamal wants to support and lets Ellis know that as well.

Jamal says, "Ellis, everything is going to be just fine. Moving out there may be a blessing in disguise, and I know it's tough to see that now, but I think you should embrace it and build on a relationship with your dad. If I had that opportunity, I would love it."

Ellis says, "You're right, bro. It's just hard for me to get past certain things my dad has said and done to me, but he is trying to work on our relationship, and I owe it to myself to appreciate him for that."

Jamal says, "We can't take people for granted regardless of their relationship to us. We get some comfortable with knowing someone will always be there that we lose sight of people being here one day and gone the next. One thing my grandma would always tell me is, "you have to appreciate your loved ones, of course, you're going to get mad at them and vice versa but don't ever take anyone for granted."

Ellis says, "Thanks for being a great friend, a brother and someone I can truly lean on for support. How in the world did you get so mature? We are only fourteen, bro!"

Jamal laughs and says, "The things I've experienced have truly helped me develop into a young man that understands I have to be able to forgive and understand why. Forgiveness is a tough thing, especially if you can't even have a conversation with the person you need to forgive. But that's when you have to look within yourself and understand you can't grow and evolve if you're stuck on something you can't control. I couldn't control who my parents were. I couldn't control if they wanted to be in my life or not, but what I could control was how I responded to all of that and if I was going to allow that to hold me back or not. My grandma was so amazing and helped me understand all of that. I would be lying if I said I don't ever wonder about certain things about my parents, but I don't dwell on them. I accept it for what it is right now at this moment. I hope you're able to forgive your dad and really allow yourself to move past that hurt and that anger. As your friend, I am telling you that you can do it, and I am looking forward to you being able to do it and us talking about it, whether it's a day from now, a month from now, or even a year from now. It is important for you to realize what you want to gain from it and put all of your energy and focus on that, whatever that might be. Just know you have people like me that are going to have your back and always support you."

Ellis says, "I appreciate you, and I thank you for the encouragement. It is definitely needed and wanted."

Jamal responds and says, "I missed Sabrina's call, and I need to call her back but call me if you need anything. I mean anything."

Chapter Eight

Jamal calls Sabrina back. The phone rings two times before she answers, full of joy and excitement. "Jamal, Jamal, I am so glad you called me back. I have some more great news! My dad is coming to visit and wants to meet you! I told him about you, and he said he's looking forward to meeting you."

Jamal says, "I can't wait to meet him, and I am honored that you told him about me. When is he coming? Do you know how long he will be staying? I am so excited for you; I know you've been waiting a long time for this moment, and it couldn't have come at a better time. I just got off of the phone with Ellis, and it seems like he's moving to Houston to live with his dad."

Sabrina says, "I'm not sure of the exact dates he is coming, also not sure of how long he will be staying. Ellis is moving to Houston. Why?!"

Jamal says, "Oh, ok, I see. He doesn't want to go, but I encouraged him to embrace it and try to build a relationship with his dad because it is a great opportunity, and I would love to be able to build a relationship with my dad, regardless of the past and what has happened or hasn't happened, healing is so necessary and needed for your personal growth."

Sabrina says, "Wow! You have such an amazing perspective. I am so thankful he has you as a friend and someone that will encourage him to be a greater version of himself. I'm sure he appreciates you so much. I know I do!"

Jamal says, "Thank you, but back to your dad coming. What

is the main thing you're looking forward to doing with him or saying to him?"

Sabrina responds, "That is a great question, and I don't have an answer for either right now, but a lot of the things he said over the phone really helped me understand a lot, and I appreciate him for speaking his truth. No matter how hurtful it may have been for me to hear it, I will never excuse him for not being around, but I have forgiven him."

Jamal says, "I am so proud of you for taking that step to forgive him and also to hear him out despite how tough it was to do so. Going to therapy helped you just as much as it helped me, and I am glad you encouraged me to come with you and to think I almost didn't go in that room. Do you and your mom have any more sessions with Dr. Sharice? If so, what else did you want to talk to her about?"

Sabrina responds, "I am so glad you went as well; I knew you needed to receive some help and understand your true greatness. Yes, we have one more session, but my mom wants to go in alone with Dr. Sharice, which I highly encourage and respect. I don't know what she wants to talk to her about, but I am glad she is communicating and wanting to communicate about whatever it may be. I am looking forward to her being able to release herself from whatever it may be, and I know she is ready to do it, which makes me happy. I just wonder what it is, and I am beginning to think more and more about it."

Jamal says, "Your mom has earned trust from me, she has good intentions, and I don't think they should be questioned just from the outside looking in. Of course, I definitely understand you are concerned about it, but I think her recognizing her needing some one-on-one support should be commended and respected on every level.

After all, most people her age are stuck in their ways and refuse to see a different way."

Sabrina says, "You know what, Jamal, you're right and thank you for providing a different perspective. I know my mom is on a journey for growth, and I will no longer question or doubt what that looks like for her. In fact, I am going to make sure she has my full support on every level."

Jamal says, "That's awesome, Sabrina! You're going to add so much value to her life just by being supportive and encouraging."

*****

Sabrina goes into her mom's room to give her a hug. As she is holding her, she begins to cry tears of joy. Sabrina's mom pulls away once she notices her crying and says, "What's wrong, Brina," a nickname she gave her.

Sabrina says, "Nothing, mom. I'm just so proud of you for being the best mom you can be despite everything, and I'm glad you want to have a one-on-one with Dr. Sharice. And I know how necessary that is for you, and I want you to know I have your back just like you've had mine, mom."

Sabrina's mom calls Dr. Sharice and schedules her last session. Dr. Sharice asks her if she will be coming alone or with her daughter. She responds and says, "I'll be coming alone. I think it is important for me to speak to you without my daughter present so I can let it all out without having to worry about her feelings and how what I say may or may not affect her."

On Saturday morning, Sabrina's mom heads to Dr. Sharice's

office, full of joy and excitement. As she is on the way there, Sabrina calls her and asks her when she will be back home. She responds and says, "I'll be back in about two or three hours. Why is everything alright?"

Sabrina responds and says, "Yes, mom, everything is perfectly fine just wanted to see what time you would be back." The reason Sabrina wanted to know is that she wanted to invite Jamal over and spend some time with him.

Sabrina's mom arrives at the office and quickly wants to share what has been on her mind for the past few sessions. Dr. Sharice asked her how she was doing, and then her mom went right in and didn't waste any time. "Dr. Sharice, I need your help. How should I approach this situation with Keith, my child's father? I can't deny that I am excited for them to finally have a relationship, but I think I still have feelings for him and don't know if I should."

Dr. Sharice responds and says, "I want you to validate your feelings. There's nothing wrong with still loving a man even though he may have done you wrong. I encourage you to have a conversation with him about it. What would be the best-case scenario and worst case? It is a strong possibility that he will feel the same way you do. Have you given some thought to that idea?"

Sabrina's mom says, "Thank you for asking those questions. I'm not sure what I would want the best-case scenario to be. The worst-case scenario would be him denying my feelings for him and brushing it off, similar to what he did in the past."

Dr. Sharice says, "I find it interesting that you were able to verbalize the worst-case scenario but didn't even give way to the best-case scenario. Why do you think that is?"

Sabrina's mom says, "I didn't even realize I did that. But I think it is because I don't expect him to feel the same way, and I don't want to get my hopes up only to then be let down yet again."

Dr. Sharice says, "That is understandable, but you owe it to yourself to always create the universe you want. What I mean by that is focusing on what you want to happen versus focusing on what you don't want to happen. I can identify with that mindset because I used to think the same way; why do I deserve this? I don't think I am ready for this. It's going to be too hard. These are some of the things I would say because I was too scared to believe I deserved everything I wanted and desired. Once I got out of that mindset, everything began to change, literally everything. It can happen to you too, but you have to believe it will and can. I believe it can and will happen for you, but you have to see for yourself, and that vision needs to be so clear."

Sabrina's mom looked and Dr. Sharice and said, "Thank you for those words of encouragement. I needed to hear that. I am going to put much more energy and focus into things I want to happen, in every aspect of my life and not just my love life. I am looking forward to talking to Keith and also letting my daughter know how I feel and not hiding from her any longer. I don't think she has any idea about how I feel about her dad. I would be surprised if she knew. He will be visiting us in a few weeks, and I am nervous and unsure of what to expect from the relationship with my daughter to the relationship with me."

Dr. Sharice says, "I don't want you to get caught up in things you can't control. That is the easiest way to cause destruction and confusion. He is not the same person you once knew and vice versa. I strongly believe people can change as long as they recognize it and want to do it, and from what you have said about Keith, it seems like he has made a conscious effort to do just that. Also, I think you have been just as conscious about changing as well, and you should be acknowledged for that. I am proud of you, woman to woman."

Tears began to well up in Sabrina's mom's eyes. She said, "Thank you so much for all of your support, I do not take it for granted, and I will not continue to see myself as undeserving. I never realized how my mindset was detrimental to my mental and emotional happiness."

Dr. Sharice recommends her to practice self-love and explains to her what that is. Self-love is doing whatever makes you happy and taking time by yourself to love on yourself and fill yourself up with words of affirmation, taking trips, reading or writing, meditating, etc. It is so many different ways to practice self-love, and as you get more and more comfortable with the act of it, more and more things will come to your mind that will encourage that self-love."

Chapter Nine

Meanwhile, back at Sabrina's mom's house, Sabrina was trying to get Jamal to come over and hang out with her, but Jamal denied it because he didn't feel comfortable being there without her mom present or at least knowing about him being over. Sabrina was growing frustrated with Jamal because she hadn't seen him in a few weeks, and she didn't understand why that was. Jamal and Ellis have been so focused on their business idea that neither of them has made much time for socializing with their other friends. They're having a hard time finding that balance, which is understandable.

Jamal tells Sabrina, "I miss you and can't wait to see you, but I don't want to disrespect your mom's house by coming over without her knowing and, more importantly, without her supervision. Did you ask your mom if it was alright for me to come to see you?"

Sabrina responds and says, "No, I didn't ask her because I know she's going to say no."

Jamal says, "Well, if you know she's going to say no, why would you want to sneak me other there and put us both in an uncomfortable situation."

Sabrina says, "My mom won't even know you were here. She's with Dr. Sharice and will be there for at least 2-3 hours," she said. "So you would be gone by the time she got back."

Jamal says, "I'd feel more comfortable hanging out with you when your mom is home. Thanks for the invite, though."

Sabrina couldn't quite understand why he wouldn't want to

spend time with her without her mother being present. After all, most young men would've jumped at the thought of that happening, but not Jamal. He respects Sabrina and her mom.

When Sabrina's mom arrived back home from her session, she saw Sabrina sitting out on the porch waiting for her. Once she pulled into the driveway, Sabrina ran to the car and opened her mom's door and pulled her out of the car. She was both excited and nervous to hear about what they talked about. Sabrina's mom says, "Hold on, Sabrina, let me get in the house", as she smiles with excitement.

Sabrina asks her mom, "How did it go?"

Her mom responds and says, "It went great! I feel empowered to be able to have a long-overdue conversation with your dad. Dr. Sharice talked to me about self-love and ways I can express being in love with myself so much more, and I am looking forward to making those things happen. I can't wait to talk to you about it and show you what it looks like as well."

Sabrina asks, "Can I know what you wanted to talk to her about in private? I'm just really curious."

Her mom responded and said, "Yes, of course, I wanted to talk to her about the feelings I still have for your dad and how I'm going to express those feelings when he comes to visit."

Sabrina looked at her mom with disbelief but also excitement. She did not expect her mom to say that at all. Sabrina says, "Really, mom, you still have feelings for him?! I can't, honestly. I'm not too surprised. I think you should go make it happen, mom, and don't hold anything back. I know you would tell me the same thing. I fully support it, and in any way, I can help, let me know, and I will be glad to do so. What do you think his response is going to be?"

Her mom responds and says, "Thank you, Brina. You saying that means a lot to me. I don't know what his response is going to be, but it is more about me telling him how I feel versus him reciprocating those feelings. I need to fully free myself one way or the other, I do want to be with him, but he feels differently; I can't do anything but respect it. Dr. Sharice talked about how it is important for me to communicate what I want and don't put much energy into what he will say or do after I do so. Dr. Sharice is truly an awesome woman, and I'm happy we got a chance to talk to her and learn from her."

Sabrina says, "I couldn't agree more mom, your feelings are valid, and my dad would be lucky to have you back in his life. Dr. Sharice was really amazing, and I am looking forward to talking to her about our growth."

*****

A few weeks have passed, and Keith and Sabrina's mom have been spending a lot of time talking on the phone and just reminiscing a lot about their past. It was a Saturday afternoon when Keith called Sabrina and asked if he could speak to her mom. He wanted to tell her about how he felt about her and how he wanted to rebuild a romantic relationship with her. Similar to Sabrina's mom, he was also nervous and excited. He had been encouraging himself for days leading up to that day.

"What's up? This is Keith. Do you have a few minutes to talk?"

Sabrina's mom says, "Yes, I do! What's on your mind?"

Keith says, "I wanted to let you know how much I appreciate

you and how much I've missed you."

Sabrina's mom sits up and says, "I appreciate you too, and you said you had missed me? I have missed you too, and you have always been on my mind."

Keith says, "Not only have I missed you, but I have also been thinking about what it would be like if we didn't break up or if we didn't end the way we did. I say all of that to say I love you, and I want to give us another try. I think it would be so much better now that we are both wiser and much more mature. What are your thoughts on that?"

She smiles and says, "Wow, I can't believe we were on the same page because I was truly thinking the same things. As a matter of fact, I just had a conversation with my therapist about having a conversation with you about my feelings for you and how they have never really faded. It is so refreshing to know that I was thinking that all by myself, and thank you for opening up to me about your current feelings. That means a lot to me. I would love for us to give it another try for the same reasons you have mentioned. I'm just so happy that we could go through what we have gone through and still be in love with one another like we are."

Keith says, "I love how the universe works and how our thoughts can be aligned with someone we are in love with. You are an amazing woman, and I am thankful to have a child with you and also to share this love with you."

Sabrina overhears the conversation and can't help but be filled with joy and excitement because she is seeing something she has always wanted to see, which is seeing a man love her mom like she deserves to be loved. Not only that, but seeing that love come from her father.

Sabrina and Connie both have healed from the past and have made the conscious decision to let go. Have they both been hurt by Keith? Yes, they have, but fortunately, they have chosen not to dwell on it, and of course, Keith has made it easier for them not to with his level of vulnerability and transparency. It was great to see Keith show that level of vulnerability because it shows Sabrina that men are capable of it and can express how they feel without being judged or ridiculed.

Connie asks Keith if he wants to talk to Sabrina about it even though she overheard the conversation, and Keith says, "Yes, I want to have a conversation with my baby girl about what just happened, and I want to hear how she feels about it. I am in a great place mentally and emotionally, and I want that to be on full display, and hopefully, it is. It is important for her to hear how I feel from me instead of her assuming anything even though it is what she may want."

Connie responds and says, "I couldn't agree more. When are you planning on coming to visit?"

Keith responds and says, "I will be there tomorrow afternoon. I booked my flight about a week ago! I wanted to surprise you and Sabrina."

Connie says, "Sounds great! I will be at the airport to pick you up, but I won't tell Sabrina so she can be fully surprised. What are some things you want to do when you come out here?"

Keith says, "My only plans are to be with you and my daughter, I have a lot of catching up to do, and I relish the opportunity to be able to do just that. What does your work schedule look like for that week?"

Connie says, "Luckily, I have my own business, I am a hairstylist, so I will reach out to my manager and let her know I will be out for that week. This is my tenth year of being in business for myself which is definitely a milestone."

Keith says, "That is amazing, and I am happy for you and your success. I also have my own business, which is a barbershop. Look at how the universe works! I have been in business for a little over six years. I have fifteen barbers."

Connie says, "Wow, I am equally as happy for you as you are for me!"

Keith says, "What does Sabrina think about your business?"

Connie says, "She's always asking questions about it from how it operates to who does what, when do they do it, why they do it, etc. She definitely has an interest in owning her own business. She just isn't sure what that would be yet, but I always tell her she has time to find out what she is passionate about so that way, it never feels like work. I don't feel like I have worked one day since I had my own salon. I love my location as well; it is in the heart of Ladera Heights, which has become an affluent African American suburb. The support I receive from the area has been amazing, and I don't take it for granted."

Keith responds and says, "I'm glad you're happy doing what you want and being in a location where you want to be. As for me, I am also in a great location in Seattle, Washington, similar to yours actually, very similar. As a matter of fact, it's so similar it's scary," as he laughs out loud. Building wealth starts when both the mother and the father understand what it takes to do so and make the necessary sacrifices for it all to come together, and with the information that was shared, both Keith and Connie feel confident that they will be able to add to each other's business in the days, months and years to come.

Chapter Ten

At this point, Sabrina had no idea her dad was coming this weekend; she began to ask her mom if she knew when he was coming and fortunately, her mom was able to hold in the secret despite how hard it was to do so. Connie says, "You should call your dad and ask him what date he is for sure coming."

Sabrina says, "You don't think he's going to flake, do you, mom?"

Connie says, "I hope he doesn't, but no, I don't think he will. Based on the conversations you've had with him, it doesn't seem like he will, and I will be surprised if he did."

Sabrina says, "Yea, your right mom, I have to be more positive and not assume the worst or assume something is going to happen that I don't want to happen."

Connie says, "I remember my grandmother told me a long time ago that our thoughts become things and to be careful with what we put into the universe, whether it be verbally or with our actions. My grandmother was a wise woman, a lot of things she would tell me I didn't understand at the moment, but as I matured and got older than began to make more and more sense. Her favorite saying was, always do your part regardless of how difficult it might be. You're going to have to swallow your pride sometimes but just know it will be worth it."

Sabrina says, "Thanks, mom, I appreciate those words of wisdom and encouragement. I'm going to give my dad a call to check in with him and see when he is coming to visit."

Sabrina calls her dad, "What's up! I just wanted to check in with you and see when you were coming to visit?"

Keith responds and says, "I'll be coming to visit you very soon, and I will let you know the exact dates in the days to come, but I am coming for sure. I don't want you to think I'm not coming or be concerned about it. But I do want to talk to you about the conversation I had with your mom. I told her I wanted to be the one to talk to you about it. As you know, she and I had a relationship in the past prior to you being born, and I let her know how much I missed her and how I wanted us to work on our romantic relationship and not just a relationship where we are co-parenting. Luckily to my surprise, she wanted the same thing, and that made me so happy to hear how she still felt about me after all of these years and after me being completely absent from her life. How do you feel about her and I giving it another try?"

Sabrina says, "Wow, dad, I am glad you told her how you felt, and I am also glad that she felt the same way, I feel great about it, but I am a little confused. You guys are going to have a long-distance relationship? I heard those rarely work out."

Keith says, "That's a great question, Sabrina, the plan is for her and I to live in the same city and state, so that way, it makes it much easier for her and me to be in a relationship because you are right long-distance relationships are hard and often don't work out because of the distance between the two people in a relationship. But I wanted to let you know all of that, and I will talk to you more about it in person because your mom will be present as well. I don't just want it to be only me talking to you about it."

While Sabrina is on cloud nine from hearing that her dad and her mom are trying to rebuild their relationship along with her finally getting a chance to build one with him, Jamal was dealing with his own issues with trying to locate his dad, with all of that going on he still did not let that affect his schooling, he still was able to maintain a 4.0 GPA for his entire freshman year. Before entering his sophomore year, he had a lot of questions he had for his biological family, but he had no real way of getting any answers up to that point. The only person he could think of that would have any information would be is god mom, but he was a bit hesitant to ask despite them having an open and honest relationship.

Jamal went on a jog to clear his mind. Upon returning, his god mom saw he had something on his mind, and she also felt his energy, so she asked him, "Is everything alright, Jamal?"

Jamal replied and said, "Actually, no, everything is not alright, I have some things on my mind, and it stems from my good friends Ellis and Sabrina and how they both have been able to seek out relationships with their fathers, and I have not been able to because I literally don't know anything about him. I was hoping you would be able to tell me anything you might know about him, if anything."

His god mom looks at him, smiles, and says, "I'm happy for your friends, and I'm also happy for you for finally inquiring about him. I honestly didn't think you cared, which was concerning, but I also didn't want to force you to do anything you didn't want to do. Your grandma made me promise her to not ever force you to do anything like that before she passed away, and I gladly made that promise to her. But your dad was a good man. When your mom passed away, he had a hard time dealing with that grief, and because he didn't properly deal with it, he distanced himself from you and everyone else. Not making any excuses for him, but I can only imagine what that did to him. Before she passed away, he was very much in your life. You had to have been about five months old when your mom passed away."

Jamal says, "I wish I could remember some things about her and him, so I had something to keep me inspired, but at times I do feel unloved. I don't like that I have those feelings at times, but I also can't continue to ignore them and not allow myself to feel them. I often wonder why my dad has never tried to find me, and I also wonder if he even remembers me. At times, I don't think he cares, and other times it's like I can feel his energy, it's hard for me to explain, but it happens from time to time. I have been trying to be patient and wait, but my patience is slowly turning into resentment, and I don't like that feeling."

She responds and says, "Jamal, I completely understand why you feel the way you do; I am going to reach out to some of his friends because I still have their phone numbers, and hopefully, those numbers still work. You're a great young man, and you deserve to be able to have those questions you have answered, and I look forward to that day when that happens. Come here, son" she opened her arms to give him a much-needed hug.

After that conversation with his god mom, Jamal did feel better, especially after they had a much-needed embrace. Jamal says, "I miss my grandma so much", as tears begin to form in his eyes.

His god mom says, "Don't hold your tears back, son, let them out, pour out. You need to let it out, and this is the best way. There's nothing wrong with showing emotion. It is healthy and necessary on every level. Even though I am older than you, you have taught me so much in this short amount of time. It is unbelievable."

Jamal responds and says, "Thank you, I really appreciate those kind words and words of encouragement despite my current circumstances. I have also learned so much from you as well, the example that you and my grandma have shown me with how to be vulnerable, why it is important to be vulnerable, and you guys saying it is always a great time to display any level of vulnerability. When I was first introduced to the word, I thought it was something I would have a hard time doing, simply because I never knew or paid attention to how easy it is to communicate how something made or makes me feel. It isn't easy, but it's much easier to do now versus when the word was first introduced to me."

His god mom responds and says, "For you to be fourteen, almost fifteen years old, and you are comfortable with communicating your feelings is really amazing. I know grown men who would rather suppress their feelings and use that energy to attract negativity. I encourage you to continue to be comfortable with evolving and maturing, also encourage your friends to do the same, and continue to lead by example. I'm aware of the conversation you had with Ellis, I overheard it, and I was not only impressed but I was also inspired by you and his conversation."

Jamal responds and says, "Thank you, I am trying to be the best person I can be despite what I am going through. Plus, I know if the shoe was on the other foot, Ellis would be just as supportive, if not more supportive. My goal was to get him to see all of the positive things that the situation could bring. Hopefully, I was able to do just that, and by the looks of it, I was able to do so. I let him know he was lucky to have his dad ready and willing to have him move to Houston. He not only gets to build a relationship with his dad but also meets his other siblings. It's a win-win, in my humble opinion."

Chapter Eleven

As the summer is coming to an end, Jamal and Sabrina both look forward to their sophomore year in high school. They talked about all of the extracurricular activities they would be interested in doing, teachers they would want to have, and subjects they would want to take on as sophomores. But before that happens, Keith is finally on his way to see Sabrina and Connie. Sabrina has no idea he is on his way.

On the way to the airport, all Keith could think about was how excited he was and how nervous he was all at the same time. He called Connie just before he boarded his plane heading to LAX, "What's up, Connie? I am officially on my way. Sabrina still doesn't know I am coming, right? I really want to surprise her."

Connie responds and says, "She has absolutely no clue at all! I am looking forward to seeing you and your daughter interact, it is something I have been meditating about for a long time, and it will be great to see it all come to fruition."

Keith says, "Great! Seems as if you and I have been meditating about the same thing," as he laughs out loud. "I am so nervous; I do not know what to expect, but I do know I am going to be exactly where I want to be, and that is with you and Sabrina."

Connie says, "My sentiments exactly, we have all come a long way, and now we get to start a new journey, but this time all together as one family."

Keith says, "I am about to board my plane now. I will call you as soon as I touch down at LAX."

Connie says, "Sounds good. See you soon".

Sabrina spoke to her dad about two hours before Connie did, and the conversation was so great. Sabrina told her mom that she couldn't wait to see him, but when she asked him when he was coming, he said, "Soon, baby girl, very soon."

Connie responds and says, "You have to give him time, sweetie, and we have to be patient; I understand why you are growing more and more frustrated, though. I believe him when he told you soon, very soon."

Sabrina says, "Alright, mom, I won't complain about it again."

With Keith not scheduled to land at LAX until 7 PM, Connie asked Sabrina if she wanted to go get ice cream from their favorite ice cream shop. Sabrina says, "Yes, can I invite Jamal to come with us?"

Connie says, "You sure can."

Sabrina calls Jamal to invite him, and of course, he says yes, no one can turn down ice cream from "Mr. Smith's Famous Ice Cream Shop". After picking Jamal up, they all began to talk about the ice cream they were going to get. Connie says, "I'm going to get two scoops of chocolate chip on a chocolate ice cream cone".

Sabrina says, "That sounds good, mom. I'm going to get two scoops of birthday cake ice cream."

Finally, Jamal says, "I'm going to have to try those one day, but I'm going to get one scoop of butter pecan ice cream and one scoop of strawberry shortcake ice cream."

They all love this ice cream because there are so many different flavors, and not to mention it is black-owned. Mr. Smith has had this shop since 1990, which is thirty years. Mr. Smith has eight employees, which includes: his four children, and four students in college, all of which grew up in that neighborhood. After his wife passed away early last year, he found himself spending more and more time with his kids, an ask she had of him while she was still alive. Every time they would go in there for ice cream, they see Mr. Smith still making it all from scratch.

But this time was a unique time because on this night, for the first time, they saw him teaching the college students all how to make his strawberry ice cream. Both Sabrina and Jamal were so enamored that they both asked Mr. Smith if they could do it too. To which Mr. Smith replied and said, "If it is alright with your mother than of course you can."

Sabrina looks at her mom and says, "Can we? This is a once-in-a-lifetime opportunity; we get to make ice cream with Mr. Smith!"

Connie responds and says, "Of course, you guys can. I would like to as well if I'm being honest," as she glares at Mr. Smith and smiles.

Mr. Smith says, "Next time, Ms. Connie, we are getting pretty busy right now, and I want to make sure the customers are taken care of first."

As Mr. Smith is teaching the kids, Connie gets a call from Keith, and he has asked her where they were because he was going to get dropped off. Sabrina is about to get the surprise of her life. She has no idea seeing as she is completely occupied with learning how to make ice cream with Jamal.

Sabrina yells over to her mom and says, "This is so fun! I don't know why it took us so long to ask Mr. Smith about teaching us how to make ice cream."

They both found themselves not only just making ice cream

but also getting to know Mr. Smith in a different way, from where he grew up, how he grew up, some of his favorite things to do when he was younger, his kids, his wife, it seemed as if Mr. Smith wanted to tell them about his whole life story. He was also interested in them and began asking both of them questions about their futures, ownership but not just ownership but the importance of it. Jamal was apprehensive about talking to him about his long-term goal which was having his own real estate company. In the midst of all of that, he was still able to teach them how to make ice cream, step by step, not missing a beat.

He says, "Just because I am considered to be old does not mean I feel old."

Sabrina asks him, "How did you start making ice cream, and do you really love doing it, or do you just do it because it comes easy to you?"

Mr. Smith says, "Those are all really good questions. I love serving the community. I love being an inspiration for upcoming black entrepreneurs. Fortunately, I was able to do all of that by doing what I love, which is making ice cream. I wanted people to think of me when they thought about ice cream. I wanted Mr. Smith and ice cream to be synonymous. All in all, I think I was able to achieve that goal. I am an eighty-one-year-old man, and I can honestly say I have lived a great life, and I wouldn't change it for anything. My advice for you both will be live life without regrets, don't let anyone tell you what you can and can't do, and never ever, ever give up on yourself and your dreams because remember, you can do anything you want to do as long as you stay focused."

Both Jamal and Sabrina were completely locked in on

everything Mr. Smith was saying, word for word. Connie walks out to meet Keith, and she asked him to park a block away from the ice cream shop so Sabrina couldn't see him. Connie greets Keith with a huge hug and then follows that with another huge hug and a warm smile. Keith picks her up and spins her around, and then whispers in his ear that he missed her and loved her. Connie smiled at him and said she missed and loved him too. As Keith and Connie are walking to the ice cream shop, Keith tells Connie that he is nervous and scared, and unsure of what to expect when he sees Sabrina. Connie reassures him that she will be excited to see him and that she has no idea he is coming. In fact, she's making ice cream with the owner and probably forgot I walked out.

As they get closer, Connie tells Keith to "Take a deep breath and relax. You're about to surprise your baby girl, all the conversations you guys have had up to this point were preparing you both for this moment."

Keith says, "You know what, you're right! Thank you for the encouragement and helping me understand how great this moment is going to be and for helping me embrace it."

Connie says, "No problem, and just to let you know, Jamal is here with us, so you're going to meet him too."

Keith responds and says, "That should be great! I know he is going to be extremely happy for Sabrina. She has spoken so highly of him."

Meanwhile, Jamal and Sabrina are learning how to make ice cream with Mr. Smith, Sabrina walks to the restroom and realizes her mom was still out, but she didn't think anything of it. Keith enters the ice cream shop with Connie and says, "Sabrina, my baby girl! Come give your dad a hug!" Sabrina looks at Jamal and her mom, smiles, and says, "Daddy is that you?! Wait, is this really happening?! It definitely is really happening. I can't believe it, mom, did you know he was coming?" as she asks these questions with so much excitement and nervousness in her voice. Sabrina says, "I don't even know where to begin, mom. Why didn't you tell me he was coming" as she smiles.

Connie says, "We wanted to surprise you, well, it was your dad's idea, and I thought it was a great one, so I supported it 100%. I know you've been wondering and anticipating his arrival, but you don't have to wonder or anticipate anymore. He's here!"

Keith looks at his daughter and says, "I've missed you so much, and you look beautiful, just like your mom, thank you for allowing me in your life because you could've said you wanted no parts of me. I would've completely understood. It feels good to be here in both you and your mom's presence. I am so excited, and I have been looking forward to this moment for such a very long time, and I apologize it took so long."

Sabrina says, "I am at a loss for words, at least right now at this moment, I am just filled with joy and excitement, dad, you're really here! I know I said that already, but I can't help it." Sabrina looks at Jamal and Mr. Smith and says, "I am in complete shock and really can't believe he's here. I really had no idea he was coming this soon to visit us. Jamal and Mr. Smith, I'd like you both to meet my dad, Keith. Dad, Jamal is the young man I was telling you about, and Mr. Smith is the owner of this ice cream shop and has been for the past thirty to thirty-five years."

Keith says, "Yes, I remember us talking about Jamal, and I also really appreciate how highly you spoke about him," as he looks

Jamal in his eyes and shakes his hand, "Nice to finally meet you, young man," then he turns to Mr. Smith and says, "Nice to meet you too, thank you for your love and support of this community, I know this is our first time meeting, but I want you to know this doesn't go unnoticed or unappreciated."

Keith is just filled with so much admiration and appreciation for this moment and doesn't want to ever forget it. Mr. Smith asks Keith if he wants to come to make ice cream with his daughter, and of course, he says yes! While explaining the details to Keith about how to make ice cream, Connie thought this would be a great moment to take some pictures, and so she did just that. Then she thought to herself, this would be a great moment for me to join them, so she gave Mr. Smith a look and asked him if she could do so after he previously told her that this opportunity would just be for the kids because the store happened to be much busier earlier when she originally asked.

So, there they were, making ice cream and laughing and smiling as if they had spent their whole lives with one another, with Jamal taking pictures of them. Once their ice cream was made, they decided to go on a walk to eat and enjoy the ice cream they all made from scratch. Keith reaches for Connie's hand so he could hold it while doing so. Sabrina reached for his hand so she could hold his. After doing so, they all looked at one another and started laughing because it was such a coincidence.

Jamal is so thankful he is able to see what love looks like a feels like from parents to children and vice versa, he just doesn't want this moment to end, and he wants to be able to enjoy every second. Jamal has gained so much love and respect for Sabrina and her mom and dad. He sees her in a completely different light, mainly because he's never seen her be so vulnerable and transparent with her feelings and not just that but expressing those feelings as well. Sabrina is still shocked by her dad coming to visit, and she's so glad she can now do the small things with him like hold his hand, eat ice cream with him, ask him questions and actually be able to see and feel his energy.

Connie shares those same sentiments, especially being able to see and feel his energy and how different that energy is now from when they first met fifteen years ago. Connie whispers in Sabrina's ear, "Ask your dad whatever you need to ask him so you can get the information straight from him. He is looking forward to not only answering your questions but also asking you questions as well."

Sabrina responds and says, "I don't want to focus on anything I want to know right now but more so just appreciate this great moment for what it really is. I am so happy mom, thank you for all that you do, and thank you for being a great mom."

As Jamal is listening to her, he begins to shed some tears, tears of pure joy. He didn't want anyone to see him crying, so he turned his back and wiped his tears on his shirt, and turned back around as if nothing had happened. Sabrina winked at him to let him know she saw him turn around and wipe his tears. He winks and smiles right back at her, he instantly feels more connected to her, and he wanted to make sure he communicated that to her. He convinced himself right then at that moment wasn't the best time, and he probably was right. He wanted her to enjoy every second with her mom and dad, and he didn't want to interfere with that in any way, shape, or form. Keith couldn't be happier; he has his daughter holding one hand and his future wife holding his other hand.

In Keith's eyes, he never knew what perfect was or if perfect existed until he was in this moment. For the first time in his life, he viewed a woman as a wife and not just someone he could love but now someone he wanted to spend the rest of his life with. In fact, he's going to talk to Sabrina about it and get her thoughts. He wants to make sure he has her full support.

Chapter Twelve

Jamal was so happy for Sabrina. He was also at an all-time high emotionally because he felt inspired to actually write his dad at the address he had, him being able to feel that energy and love from a family was just what he needed to reach out to his family. He couldn't wait to get home and share the news with his god mom and also give Ellis a call and tell him. With their second year of high school vastly approaching, he wanted to start the year off in a way he had never been able to start school off, which was communicating with family members. Seems like such a small thing because most kids his age have the privilege of being able to see their moms and dads frequently. But before he wrote his dad, he wanted to talk to Sabrina and get some advice from her, and he also wanted to hear about the rest of her experience with her dad.

He gives Sabrina a call, and when she answers the phone, he says, "What's up, Sabrina! I wanted to check on you and see how you were doing and also ask you a few questions."

Sabrina says, "Hi Jamal! I am doing great, thanks for asking. How are you doing?"

Jamal says, "I am glad you're doing great; I am doing good as well. I wanted to get your advice on me reaching out to my dad. Do you think it is a good idea? I was going to write him a letter since my god mom was able to get an address on him."

Sabrina says, "Wow! Yes, I think it is a great idea to write him, definitely do it! And if you need or want help, I would love to help you."

Jamal says, "Thank you, Sabrina, I am just really nervous and unsure of what to expect, and I would love to take you up on that offer of you wanting to help me write him. I will let you know when I plan on writing him, but it will be within the next few days."

Sabrina says, "Sounds good to me, and I am so proud of you for taking that step. I can only imagine how tough that is to do!"

Jamal says, "Thank you for your undying support. It doesn't go unnoticed or underappreciated."

Now that Jamal knows he has Sabrina's support with writing his dad, he now wants to create some talking points and be able to articulate himself in a way that he doesn't come off angry or mad, even though he is both. Something told him to ask his god mom if she was able to get a phone number on him because even though he felt more comfortable writing him, he also wanted to have to option of calling him as well. Unfortunately, she did not have a working number on him at the time, but she was committed to finding one. Feeling unwanted, underappreciated, and undervalued, Jamal has battled with the confusion of being happy for his friends, Sabrina and Ellis, or being jealous of them and their situations with their family.

Of course, he is happy for them, but the more they spend time with their families, the more he becomes confused about his circumstance with his family. Just when he thought he was ready to accept his family not being a part of his life, it became that much harder when the friends were able to not only spend time with their families but also be appreciated. It has been a constant battle for him and a battle he wants to be able to win, and so he plans on doing just that.

Keith was eager to have a heart-to-heart conversation with

Sabrina about the relationship he was looking forward to building with Connie. He asks Sabrina, "Do you have a few minutes so I can talk to you?"

Sabrina says, "Of course," she doesn't have a clue what he wants to talk to her about, but she was eager to hear.

Keith says, "I want to talk to you about asking your mom to marry me and spend the rest of her life with me, I've waited long enough, and I don't want to wait any longer. What are your thoughts on me asking for her hand in marriage?"

Sabrina smiles and says, "Really, dad?! I think that's great, and I fully support it 100%! How are you going to do it, and when do you plan on doing it? And I just thought about it. I get to be a part of a surprise on her," as she laughs with extreme excitement. "I would love to see you propose to my mom."

Keith says, "I have a plan, and when the time gets closer, I will begin to fill you in. Thank you for your support; it really means a lot. Yes, you get to surprise her and get her right back", as he says while he is laughing out loud. Keith says, "I want to make this night very special for her, and I plan on doing just that; she deserves it! Of course, I plan on talking to her about marriage and making sure our ideas align, which I think they do, but I definitely don't want to assume. There's more information I need to gather from her in order to make this night super special for all of us. I am so nervous and excited, Sabrina."

Sabrina says, "No need to be nervous, dad, you're going to do great, and she's going to really appreciate whatever plan you have, and so will I. Thank you for sharing this with me. I can wait to see it all happen and come to fruition."

Sabrina now has something else to look forward to talking to Jamal about, and she can't wait to do that either. She is so happy about how her summer is turning out and can't believe it. But in the back of her mind, she is still concerned about Jamal and if he will be able to communicate with his dad. And for that reason, she is a bit hesitant to share the good news she has because she doesn't want her news to make him feel more pressure than he already does or that she assumes he does.

Sabrina is hesitant to ask Jamal if he feels pressure with finding his dad and hearing back from him, mainly because she knows she would feel that pressure if the roles were reversed. She wanted to get some advice from her mom, but she couldn't let her know what was going to happen in the months to come with her dad proposing, so instead, she turned to her dad for advice. Even though she was looking forward to asking her dad, she still was nervous about doing so. After all, she still didn't really know how her dad felt about Jamal. But before she talked to her dad about the Jamal situation, she wanted to talk to her mom about her dad and how she feels about him visiting and possibly doing more than just visiting.

Sabrina says to her mom, "Are you happy my dad is here like I am?"

Connie says, "I sure am, Sabrina, that's a random question," as she looks at her with a sarcastic smile. Connie then says, "Why do you ask that?"

Sabrina says, "Oh, no reason, mom. I just wanted to see if we were on the same page. I am so glad he is here, and he is really putting forth the effort for both of us, despite him not being in our lives for this long. Does he have any plans on moving out here permanently, or have you guys not discussed that yet?"

Connie says, "We are definitely on the same page in regard to him being out here. His presence and energy is so needed and felt. He and I have not discussed him moving out here permanently just yet, but we will, and I will be sure to make sure we include you in the conversation, Ms. Nosey."

Sabrina responds and says, "Thanks, mom! I am glad you guys are getting along and are happy in each other's presence. It really helps me and gives me a lot of confidence."

Sabrina paces back and forth in a room to think about how and when she was going to tell Jamal her great news, and she decided you know what, I am going to just tell him. Sabrina calls Jamal, "What's up, Jamal! Are you busy? I have something I want to tell you, and I am so excited to do so."

Jamal says, "What's up, Sabrina! No, I am not busy at the moment. I am all ears."

Sabrina screams, "My dad wants to marry my mom, he wants to marry her, and my mom doesn't have a clue."

Jamal says, "Wow, that is exciting, and I am excited for you and your family! When is your dad going to propose?"

Sabrina says, "He doesn't know an exact date yet, he still wants to give it some time, but he knows he wants to spend the rest of his life with her. And my mom has no clue, and I know she loves surprises because she says it all of the time. This is the surprise of all surprises."

Jamal says, "How awesome is that, not just a man, but your dad committing to your mom for the rest of his life. That is what I aspire to be like, and I will be just that, a man with a plan for my career and the woman I will love."

Sabrina is so glad that she didn't go along with her assumption, thinking Jamal would be envious or jealous. She was able to hear his support and appreciation for her mom and her dad.

Jamal loved hearing Sabrina's great news. In fact, he said to her, "I am ready to start writing my dad a letter. How do you think I should start it?"

Sabrina says, "I'm glad this day came sooner than later, Jamal. I think you should start it by saying who you are and how much you have longed to have a relationship with him. Talk to him about how you are doing without having a relationship with him, not to make him feel bad, but it is important to tell your truth despite how it might make other people feel. That's what Dr. Sharice was always encouraging us to do. Tell him how you are doing in school, let him know about your entrepreneurial aspirations, but don't be shy to say what's on your mind and talk about how your feelings are hurt."

Jamal says, "Thank you, Sabrina. I needed that advice and that encouragement. I will have this done by tomorrow night and then mail it to him. He lives in Chicago, Illinois. I am optimistic about him writing me back. I don't want to get my hopes up too high."

Sabrina says, "Jamal, I want to tell you something Dr. Sharice told my mom, and then she shared it with me. Put your energy and your thoughts into what you want to happen versus what you don't want to happen. If you want your dad to respond, don't think about him not doing it, is that going to be an easy task? Definitely not, but it is possible. After all, it happened for my mom in reference to my dad. Now that you have some talking points, I have all the confidence in the world in you, and I also believe not only will your dad respond, but he will be excited to hear from you."

Jamal says, "You're right, Sabrina, that is some great advice, and I will take that with me for the rest of my life."

Chapter Thirteen

Jamal went to go talk to his god mom and let her know he was ready to write his dad and mail it to him. As he entered her room, he hesitated because he saw her with her eyes closed, facing straight ahead, and he didn't want to interrupt. He said, "God mom, are you alright?"

She responded and said, "Yes, I am. Thanks for asking!"

Jamal said, "What were you doing?"

She said, "I was meditating, centering my thoughts and focusing on things I want to happen. For example, you are writing your dad and hearing back from him."

Jamal says, "What is meditating? And how often do you do it? Thanks for thinking of me and my dad. By the way, I've been hearing a lot of things lately about focusing on things we want to happen. Thanks for reassuring me."

She says, "The definition of meditate is to think deeply or focus one's mind for a period of time, in silence or with the aid of chanting, for religious or spiritual purposes or as a method of relaxation. I personally use it for spiritual purposes. I meditate four to five times a day, when I wake up, after I eat breakfast, after I go on my walk, after I eat lunch, and before I go to sleep. But there are times when I meditate more, but those are the consistent times."

Debra, Jamal God's mom, was glad Jamal saw her meditating because she was able to introduce something new to him and something that could relax his mind and help him center his thoughts.

Jamal says, "I think I am going to try that out. I think it can help me with a lot of different things I find myself thinking about and worrying about. I don't know if I will start out doing as much as you, but I do want to incorporate it into my everyday life. Do you think we can meditate together? Can you let me know whenever you do it, so I can join you?"

Debra says, "Of course, we can do it together. I would love that for us. It's really not hard at all. For your first time, you might feel weird initially, but once you calm yourself down and just focus on your energy and self-improvement, you will be perfectly fine."

Jamal says, "I would love to start today. I can in here to let you know that I'm going to start writing my dad today, and I'm going to mail the letter to him first thing tomorrow morning. Sabrina helped me with some talking points, and I feel like I am ready to send this to him and eagerly wait for his response. After I finish with the letter, can we mediate together?"

Debra says, "I am so happy for you, and I look forward to him responding to you. Let's meditate before you start writing him and after."

Jamal says, "I would love to!"

Jamal asks, "How long should we meditate?"

Debra says, "As long as you want to, but make sure you meditate long enough to relax your mind, body, and soul."

Jamal says, "Will do."

As they begin meditating, Jamal hears Debra saying, "You are amazing, you are beautiful, you are resilient, you are fantastic." And she kept repeating it over and over.

Those are called positive affirmations. A positive affirmation is when a person repeats to themselves how they see themselves and or how they want to be. So, once he learned about that, he decided to repeat some positive affirmations as well, "You are brave, you are peace, you are worthy, you are loved, you are wanted."

Once Jamal finished mediating, he felt more empowered and more confident in his ability to gain strength and encouragement in order to be able to finally begin writing his dad. Right before he started, he wanted to reflect on all of the things Sabrina had told him, and now he was ready to start. Once he began, he found himself amazed and surprised by how much he was not only able to write but also what he was able to write. For example, he wrote, "Dad, I love you, we all make mistakes, and I forgive you." That's how he ended his letter. He reads his letter to Debra, more so just for someone to hear it and make sure he didn't have any errors. She was so moved by what he wrote that she began crying and was unable to control her emotions, nor did she want to.

As Jamal looks up at her, he then sees how moved she is and began consoling her by holding her and hugging her as he continued to read his letter. He still didn't have a title for it, but he wasn't as concerned with that as much as he was just gathering the strength to be able to complete it. The letter was so powerful and authentic, and Debra appreciated him not being angry or upset but more so trying to gather understanding because, after all, this is his dad, and he wants to create a space of comfort so they can finally embark on a healthy relationship. The letter reads as this:

What's up, dad! I know we don't know each other, but I wanted to write this letter to you so we can begin to get to know one another. It took a lot for me to write this to you because of fear, fear that you wouldn't respond or fear that you would respond and respond saying you don't want anything to do with me. I envision us going to the parks, throwing a football around, you talking to me about girls, me talking to you about my goals and aspirations, I could go on and on. You have created a great young man, a young man that values his future, friends, family, and overall, his loved ones. I am getting ready to start the tenth grade, and I am so excited to do so. My god mom has truly been an inspiration for me. Just recently, she taught me how to meditate and how to center my thoughts. How is everything going with you? Do you meditate? If so, how often? Sorry for bombarding you with questions, but I am excited to write you and not sure how to articulate that fully. I just want you to know I love you, we all make mistakes, and I forgive you. After all, a son needs his dad, and a dad needs his son.

Sincerely, Your son, Jamal Avery Dixon.

Debra is in complete awe of Jamal because she knows how difficult writing that letter was. She's so proud of him and wants to let him know. Many times, we don't let our loved ones know we are happy for them or proud of them, but Debra wanted to make sure she not only communicated that verbally but also displayed that with action as well. And fortunately, the action she wanted to do was throw a celebration for Jamal, just a few friends, cake, and some ice cream, and since she knew he had just learned how to make ice cream at Mr. Smith's shop, she wanted to get his favorite ice cream cake from there. She called Sabrina first just to let her know and also ask her if that would be a good idea and if Jamal would appreciate it, and without hesitation, she responded, "Most definitely. Is it anything I can do to help?"

Debra responds and says, "Yes, it is actually. Can you invite your mom and dad? It doesn't have to be anything big, but us acknowledging his accomplishment would be amazing."

Sabrina said, "Of course, I am sure they would love to come and support Jamal."

They soon realized how tough it was to surprise Jamal, mainly because he was so in tune with everything. But they did not let that stop them. The reason they wanted to surprise him was that they wanted to acknowledge his efforts and let him know it didn't go unnoticed or undervalued.

Sabrina let her dad and her mom know the plans they had for Jamal, and they both lit up with excitement, not because of the surprise party but because of the letter he wrote. They both asked Sabrina if she had read the letter or heard it, and she said, "No, not yet, but I anticipate him reading it to me. I know he read it to his god mom already."

Without hesitation, they both agreed to come and show their love and support to Jamal. They all appreciate his level of strength and determination when it comes to finding his loved ones and his relentless approach in doing so. Jamal calls Sabrina and wants to thank her for her continued support but more specifically for giving him the confidence and providing him with a guideline for him to start writing. Jamal also wanted to talk to her about mediating and if she had heard of it or knew what it was. Jamal asks her, "Have you ever heard of meditating?"

Sabrina responds and says, "No, what is that?"

Jamal says, "My god mom introduced me to it, and it is when

a person repeats to themselves how they see themselves and or how they want to be. My god mom and I meditated before I wrote my dad, and after, she was saying these chants, "you are amazing, you are beautiful, you are resilient, you are fantastic." Then I felt encouraged to say my own chants, which were, "you are brave, you are peace, you are worthy, you are loved, you are wanted." Jamal goes on to say, "The feeling I received after was unexplainable. I say all that to say I encourage you to start meditating and just start envisioning things you want for you and your family."

*****

Dr. Sharice calls to check in on Connie and her family and see how things are going since they have received therapy from her. Dr. Sharice says, "What's up, Connie! How's everything going with you and your daughter?"

Connie responds and says, "Everything is going great. I really appreciate you for all of your love and support. Keith is in town visiting. Keith is Sabrina's dad, he has been here for about two weeks, and things are going great. Everything has been so peaceful and relaxing with him being here, I am happier, and Sabrina is as well. We surprised Sabrina, she didn't know he was coming as soon as he did, and if I could pay to see that look on her face again, I would. She was making ice cream at Mr. Smith's shop, and he walked right in. She saw him and was in complete shock. A few days prior, she was asking me when he was coming, and it was so hard to keep that secret from her, but I am glad we did."

Dr. Sharice says, "That is amazing. I'm glad it is working out the way you all want it to. I am not surprised at all. You put energy into what you wanted to see happen, and it happened. The universe is undefeated. I love Mr. Smith's ice cream, by the way. That was my favorite place growing up as a kid. Now that I think about it, I haven't been back in years."

Connie says, "I am proud of myself for stepping out of my comfort zone and allowing myself to be uncomfortable, and I thank you for encouraging me. We have to have an ice cream date there soon; Sabrina would love that. Would you be open to doing that, Dr. Sharice?"

Dr. Sharice responds and says, "That sounds like a great idea. Let's set up a time and day two weeks from now. How's Jamal doing?"

Connie says, "Sounds good! How does next Friday afternoon at 2 PM sound? And Jamal is doing great things. You'd be proud. I'll make sure to invite him so he can tell you all of the wonderful things he is doing to better himself."

Dr. Sharice says, "I can't wait! It will also be great to see Mr. Smith; hopefully, he can teach me how to make ice cream as well."

Connie says, "Yes, I will try to make that happen for us, an ice cream lesson from the great Mr. Smith."

Dr. Sharice responds and says, "Oh yea, one last thing, have you reached out to your parents about that trauma you went through?"

Connie says, "No, I haven't. I've been so focused on Keith and Sabrina that I either consciously or unconsciously suppressed those thoughts/feelings. But I thank you for reminding me, even though that situation is much tougher than acknowledging my feelings for Keith."

Dr. Sharice says, "It only seems easier because of the

relationship you and Keith once had and so naturally, you felt more comfortable and plus that trauma is from your childhood, which means you would have to tell your parents some things so inevitably, it's going to seem tougher and rightfully so. My suggestions would be for you to write down some talking points, practice saying them in the mirror, and practice saying them to your daughter. I think it would be very helpful for her to hear how you feel about some of your childhood and how your childhood has affected you in ways you are unaware of. What are your thoughts on that advice?"

Connie says, "Wow, thank you! I think that advice is great, and I look forward to not only implementing it but also following through with it as well. Often times I talk myself out of doing things I know would benefit me because of fear that I will hurt some feelings or make someone uncomfortable."

Dr. Sharice says, "Forget about hurting someone else's feelings. What I want you to do is focus on yourself and your feelings. No one else's feelings will matter because you need to free yourself, free yourself from that pain, that hurt, that embarrassment, I could go on and on, but you get the picture, Connie."

Connie says, "Yes, you are right. I am going to take all of your advice, and if I have any questions about anything or need any help with anything, can I give you a call?"

Dr. Sharice says, "Of course, you can. I look forward to your questions."

Chapter Fourteen

As Jamal and Sabrina start their tenth-grade year, they both are excited and nervous, excited because of the new journey they're about to embark on and nervous because they don't know what to expect. They receive their schedules and see that they have zero classes together, both of which were confused as to why that was. But as they looked at their schedules, they realized they have most of the same classes but at different times. Both feeling a lot more comfortable mainly because they had a better understanding of what to expect, at least socially.

Jamal tells Sabrina, "I think it is interesting how the social aspect of our high school experience doesn't get as much attention as the academic side of it. I see it as you can't have one without the other."

Sabrina says, "You're right, Jamal! I think it doesn't receive as much attention because that's not what we are encouraged to go to school for. But they do go hand and hand, and I think it's tough to have success with just one and not the other, depending on what your goal is for the school overall."

As Sabrina and Jamal continue to get acclimated to their new schedules, Jamal realizes his friend of five-plus years has moved to another city to be with his dad. Jamal wants to put more of an emphasis on his social experience in high school and not just academically. He plans on attending more sporting events, more school events and building relationships with his new teachers as well as his ones from his ninth-grade year. The reason he wants to do that is because he feels like school is more than just putting a lot of pressure on yourself academically but allows the social aspect of school to balance you out and not create so much stress, anxiety and impatience.

In fact, Jamal wants to create a plan for his school to start offering classes on how to deal with anxiety and stress as it relates to school and even outside of school. Even though counselors are available for students, that still only provides one hour out of a week or maybe two hours, depending on your situation or circumstance. Jamal thinks that if students can relate with each other more, then their experience can be much better. He also would like to see how his teachers navigate with their anxiety and stress as well. Sabrina thinks this is all a great idea, and she believes he will be able to come up with a plan that will get this going sooner than later.

Sabrina says, "Maybe you should just go to your counselor now and mention it; not saying having a plan isn't great, but no need to spend that time planning it when you can mention it now and then start working on the plan later. What do you think?"

Jamal says, "You know what, you're right, Sabrina. I think with me mentioning it; we can start getting the ball rolling versus me sitting back waiting while I develop some type of plan. Working together with the staff could make for a much better plan. I'm going to schedule an appointment with my counselor at the end of the school day. I would love for you to come with me if you can; if not, I understand."

Sabrina says, "That is true. I would love to come with you. Let me just make sure my mom says it is alright first."

Jamal says, "Awesome. I hope your mom and dad are alright

with you coming with me. I could really use your support."

The following day, Jamal and Sabrina visit Jamal's counselor, Mr. Reid, to express how they feel adding certain classes can and will help their classmates. Fortunately, Mr. Reid is fully on board and agrees with Jamal and Sabrina. He says, "I love this idea. Actually, I really love this idea. I think we can make this happen. The only thing is it may take a year to get in full motion."

Jamal says, "That's great! Thank you for listening to us and hearing us out. I was a little apprehensive at first because I didn't know what to expect but thank you for being supportive Mr. Reid. Is there anything you need from me moving forward?"

Mr. Reid says, "As of right now, no, but what I would like for us to do is meet at least twice a month. Is that something you can commit to?"

Jamal says, "Sounds good! I am able to meet twice a month. Just let me know the dates, and I will be there. This is important for us, and I know it will be beneficial."

Mr. Reid gives Jamal a handshake and tells him to enjoy the rest of his day. Jamal and Sabrina walk out of his office feeling great. Sabrina expresses how proud she is of him and how she's inspired by him as well. Jamal is on cloud nine, he went in feeling confident, and with his positive thoughts, he was able to act those out in his tone and energy. Positive thoughts equal positive results, as he continued to say to himself as he and Sabrina walked out of the office.

Connie comes to pick Jamal and Sabrina up from school, and she notices the huge smiles on their faces, Connie wasn't fully aware of what their meeting was about, but Sabrina and Jamal would quickly inform her once they got in the car.

Sabrina says, "Mom, mom, Jamal and I just had a meeting with Jamal's school counselor, and we talked to him about adding a class that helps students with anxiety, stress, building their confidence, and even a class on meditation and the benefits of it. He spoke with so much confidence like he knew his idea was going to get approved; it was amazing to see. Mr. Reid was so impressed with Jamal, that the meeting didn't last long at all, maybe 10 minutes. Mr. Reid is on board and can't wait to put the plan in motion. They are going to meet twice a month. Sorry, Jamal, I didn't leave anything for you to tell my mom," as she smiled at him with excitement, and then they both laughed out loud.

Sabrina's mom says, "Well, it looks like your sophomore year is off to a great start. Let me know if it is anything I can do to help."

Connie is looking forward to telling Keith this great news and does so as soon as they walk into the house, "Keith, Keith, Jamal and Sabrina just had a meeting with Jamal's school counselor, and we talked to him about adding a class that helps students with anxiety, stress, building their confidence, and even a class on meditation and the benefits of it. He spoke with so much confidence like he knew his idea was going to get approved. It was amazing to see. Mr. Reid was so impressed with Jamal that the meeting didn't last long at all, maybe 10 minutes. Mr. Reid is on board and can't wait to put the plan in motion. They are going to meet twice a month; sorry, Sabrina, I didn't leave anything for you to tell dad."

Sabrina looks at her mom and says, "Well, jeez, mom," as she laughs out loud.

Connie says, while laughing out loud, "You did the same thing to Jamal when you guys got in the car. I just reversed it," as she shrugs her shoulders. "I am so proud of those two. They inspire me and impress me more and more every day. I am so thankful and appreciative for their level of dedication to helping their generation be better and more confident with their abilities."

Keith echoes those same sentiments and adds, "They really make a great team, and it is really refreshing, he respects her, and she respects him, and with that respect for one another, you guys are able to accomplish great things case in point that meeting amongst other things, I am a proud dad."

Sabrina looks at both of them with admiration and says, "you guys inspire me, more than you both know, you both instil confidence in me and a lot of times it is unconscious to me until I have moments like this when I am able to see it in full. Thank you both for being the best you can be and for allowing me to be the best I can be."

As Sabrina is walking into her bedroom, her dad says he has something he would like to talk to her about, "let's have a seat. I know when I am going to propose to Connie, I have it all planned out. Can you make a video for her birthday? That is when it will happen, so two months from now, on November 14th."

Sabrina says, "yes, dad, I can and will make a video. What do you want me to include in that video? This is a great idea; I know she won't expect it at all. Will you be staying here until then, or will you be going back home?"

Keith says, "include how much you love her and appreciate her. We are going to celebrate her for her birthday. I don't even want her to suspect anything from your video. I will be going back home in two weeks to get myself prepared for the proposal as well as check on my businesses. They do seem to be doing great. My manager in charge has been doing a great job in my absence."

Sabrina says, "do you think I could go back with you when you go? I would love to see how your business operates as well as spend more time with you in your element."

Keith says, "I would love for you to come to visit me, but school has just started, and I don't think that it would be a good idea for you to miss so many days of school. But maybe you can come to visit for a weekend. I don't see a problem with that at all. I will talk to your mom about it, and I am sure she will love that. How does that sound, my princess?"

Sabrina says, "yes, you are right, dad. Please talk to mom about me visiting for a weekend. I would love that."

Keith says, "sure thing, baby girl."

Right after Keith has that conversation with Sabrina, he calls Connie right away to talk to her about Sabrina coming to visit him, "Connie, I think Sabrina could benefit a lot from coming to visit me, of course, it would be for a weekend, so she doesn't miss school. What are your thoughts about that?"

Connie says, "I think that is a great idea, and I fully support that. When did you want her to come visit you?"

Keith says, "not sure just yet; I'll have an answer for you and her within the next couple of weeks. We can both let her know together that she is coming to visit me. I think that it would be great if we both were present when we told her."

Connie says, "I agree. Both of us being present would send a great message and demonstrate the unity we have and how we are on the same page."

Keith and Connie called Sabrina into the living room so they could tell her the great news, but first, they wanted to talk to her about why it is important for her to see them on the same page and in sync about important decisions such as this one.

Keith says, "baby girl, I talked to your mom about you coming to visit, and we decided that it would be a great idea for you to come visit on a weekend in the near future."

Connie says, "it is definitely a great idea for you to go visit him and see outside of California as well. We wanted to both talk to you about it versus you hearing it from either myself or your dad. Are you excited?"

Sabrina says, "thanks, mom and dad. I really appreciate you both talking to me about it and showing your support. For not just going to visit my dad but spending more time with him. I am looking forward to this trip and also looking forward to visiting my dad's barbershop and seeing how it all operates."

Jamal and Sabrina continue their pursuit in creating a class in school for their peers to deal with anxiety, but instead of one class, they want to propose at least one class for each grade level. As incoming freshman, they know first-hand how overwhelming your first year of high school can be, bigger campus, more teachers, and not to forget the pressure of meeting new people, as sophomores although your first year in the book some sophomore's feel more pressure because they know now what to expect and then they are beginning to get introduced to tougher classes that look good on report cards for college, juniors are the next in line to graduate and this is when college applications are beginning to get filled out as well as visiting college campus', lastly, seniors because they are all embarking on their last year of high school and what that means is adulthood is soon to follow, and instead of practicing the SAT's and ACT's, they are taking the real tests in order to position themselves in the best position to compete for academic scholarships and not just that but to get accepted to competitive colleges, you would think people you have gone through this process would understand the pressure it puts on students and not just pressure but the anxiety it can cause. After all, most of us don't know what we want to study when we go to college or how to even understand what to study.

One thing high school does prepare you for is how to be social, most people are successful with doing so because it is natural to gravitate toward people you have things in common with. High school is a great place; unfortunately, some people drop out, but all in all, high school is great, as long as you understand how to maximize it every single day.

Jamal says, "I think if more high schools incorporated teaching skills on the importance of having the ability and the confidence to interact with their peers, students wouldn't drop out as often. As a current student, I think it is imperative that we create a curriculum focused on these things if we truly want to see progress. Making these classes happen will improve the dropout rate, and I truly think it will also help our teachers and staff as well. After all, they are human too. Asking teachers how they decompress is major. Some teachers might not even be able to find the time to do it. These are questions we should be asking and not just focusing on the academic part of high school. Now that we have somewhat of a plan in motion, now we have to figure out how to turn that plan into fruition. With the help of my counselor I know we can and will be able to do it."

Sabrina just looks at Jamal in awe of him and all of his very well-thought-out ideas. She adds, "what do you think about offering a survey to the teachers and asking them what they think the best way is to gather all of this information. I think if we can get teachers on board with all of this, it will be much easier to get the students on board."

Jamal says, "that is a great idea! We definitely need to make them feel included, and I think your idea is a great way to do that plus, they need to see support coming their way as well."

Sabrina says, "that is exactly what I was thinking, we are putting a lot of energy and effort into us as students, which we should, but we can't forget about the teachers. Without them, it would be even tougher for us. We should have your counselor mention it when all of the teachers and staff meet up. It is called Professional Development. One of my teachers mentioned it a couple of days ago."

Jamal responds and says, "yes, I will talk to him about making sure he not only mentions it but actually creates some excitement around it. You know what?! I think I should be the one who talks to the staff about it because it'll be great for them to see a current student has their back just as much as I have the student's back. Do you think that's a good idea, Sabrina?"

Sabrina looks at him with a serious face and says, "that is a great idea, Jamal! I love that, and I am hopeful that Mr. Waverly will like it as well."

Chapter Fifteen

As the weekend is approaching, Sabrina talks to her mom about going to visit her dad. Sabrina is also worried about her mom and dad changing their minds and saying it is best for her to finish the school year and wait for the summer. The reason she is concerned about that is because her mom had already mentioned it to her a few weeks ago, and she is uncertain about how to convince her that she will be able to handle going during the school year. She wants her parents to exercise some trust with her, even though she knows how hard that can be for both of them.

Connie calls Sabrina into her room to talk to her, "Sabrina, how are you feeling about going to visit your dad?"

Sabrina says, "I feel great about it. I do want to say that I think you guys should trust that I can go visit him during the school year and have faith that it won't interfere with my schoolwork at all. Why don't you guys think I can handle going to visit him during the school year?"

Connie says, "I appreciate you asking that question. We are just concerned that it will be easy for you to get distracted and how that possible distraction can make you lose focus and have a hard time getting it back."

Sabrina says, "well, mom, a wise lady once told us that it is important for us to think about things we want to happen versus things we don't want to happen. I am saying that because it seems as if you guys have already made up in your mind that it is impossible for me to be able to go during the school year, and if I am being honest, that is a bit unfair. I haven't given either of you a reason not to trust that I can handle it. In fact, I think I have given you guys reason to be able to trust it. I have maintained a 3.7 GPA, and I have been extremely responsible with how I have handled things outside of school, such as this. All I ask is that you guys give me a chance, and I will make sure neither of you will regret it, mom."

Connie says, "that is so well stated, my daughter, and you are right. You deserve a lot of credit for the way you have handled yourself, and I agree with everything you said. I am going to talk to your dad about you going to visit him in a couple of weeks."

Sabrina says, "thanks, mom! I really appreciate you for hearing me out and really listening to me. That means a lot to me. Do you think dad will be on board with it 100%?"

Connie says, "yes, I do think he will be. I am looking forward to telling him about our conversation and how well you articulated your thoughts. It really made me so proud, and in fact, I was holding back tears because my baby girl is really growing up, and it is awesome to see. I know I said I would talk to your dad about you going to visit in a few weeks, but when would you like to go visit?"

Sabrina says, "I owe it all to you mom, you have been a true inspiration to me, and you have really taught me a lot consciously or unconsciously, some things I don't think you intentionally taught to me, but I am always paying attention to you, observing how you handle so many different situations, but to answer your question, I don't mind going in a few weeks, I just didn't want to have to wait until the summertime. So, with that being said, in a few weeks would be perfect."

Both Connie and Sabrina were relieved by how each other

were supportive and how communicative they each were. Their relationship is one that they both value and appreciate. Connie calls Keith to talk to him about the conversation she and Sabrina just had and wants to get his thoughts and opinion on it as well. She tells Keith, "I know we had a talk about Sabrina not coming to visit you until the summer, and we also discussed why that was a good idea. However, I just had a talk with her, and she communicated so great and articulated herself so well about her being able to handle coming for a weekend. I was so proud of her because I could tell she put a lot of thought into everything she was saying, and she made a lot of sense. She mentioned how she has been able to maintain a 3.7 GPA throughout her year and a half in high school. She mentioned her extracurricular activities with Jamal and how they are making a difference not just for their peers but for the teachers as well. With all of that, I told her I would talk to you about her visiting in a few weeks to see what you thought."

Keith says, "that young lady never ceases to amaze me. You have done such a great job with her, and I don't think you give yourself enough credit, so I will. Connie, the way you are present in her life is truly amazing, you have taught me so much, and I don't take that for granted at all. I would be honored to have my daughter come visit in a few weeks. In fact, let's have her visit exactly two weeks from now, from Friday night to Sunday evening. I will buy her a plane ticket now. Can you call her in the room so I can be present when she hears the news?"

Connie smiles from ear to ear and says, "thank you so much, Keith. Hearing you say all of that really touched me and made me feel amazing, I just wanted to make sure Sabrina always knew she could talk to me about any and everything, and I am glad she feels like she can. She is truly a special person, and I am looking forward to seeing her continue to grow and mature into her womanhood."

Keith says, "I think as human beings we don't do a good enough job of telling the people we love, why we love them and appreciate them. Moving forward I want to make sure not only you know I love you, but you know why I love you. I have learned so much being out there with you two over the past few weeks, and I don't know if you or Sabrina really understand and truly appreciate you guys relationship. It is amazing and a joy to be around."

Connie says, "you know what, you are right, Keith; it is easy for me to get comfortable and not look at our relationship and truly see the value and appreciation for it like I should. With that being said, I'm going to have a dinner date with my daughter and express to her how much I appreciate her and our relationship. Not only do I think she will appreciate it, but she will also get a chance to hear me really let her know how much I value her and the relationship we have."

*****

Despite the success Sabrina and her family are having with their dynamics, Jamal is still longing for that relationship with his dad. His optimism seems just, and he is feeling good about hearing back from his dad. He sent the letter to him a week ago, and is patiently waiting for his response. He eagerly checks the mail every day when he gets home from school, and he knows that there will be one day when he does, and he will see that letter and rush inside to open it. But before that happens, he knows he has to exercise patience and give it some time. The only frustrating part about that is not knowing how much time it will take. But his god mom's love has truly been able to help him be patient and understanding.

With her love, he has been able to grow a different level of appreciation for her because of her patience and guidance throughout that process. She understood that she couldn't put pressure on him to do anything, but she had to guide him and be there for him when he would get discouraged or frustrated, which happened often. She would often say things like, "I am here to help guide you, I know this is tough, but you got this. I am so proud of you." I am so proud of you is a statement that is often minimized because some people deem it a cliché one. However, hearing that can and often does not only empower the person hearing it, but it also empowers the person who says it. It allows the person who is saying it to take a step back, no matter how small or big that step is, to see someone else's progress and determination for a goal or a responsibility.

Joyce recalls the time when she heard her mom was proud of her, she doesn't remember what she said it for, but she remembers how it made her feel to hear it. So, she makes a conscious effort to make sure Jamal constantly hears words of affirmations not only because he deserves them but because she wants to normalize the behavior as well. It shouldn't make anyone feel awkward or weird to hear someone else express their happiness or appreciation for a loved one. We are quick to normalize behavior that could be detrimental to us but ignore the behavior that could uplift us, and I will do everything in my power to dispel that myth.

Jamal has been conscious about making sure he provides that level of encouragement and affirmation for his friends before Ellis left to go live with his dad. He made sure to tell him he loved him and that he was proud of him and gave reasons why for both. Jamal told Ellis, "I love you, man. I am proud of you for stepping out of your comfort zone and really taking a chance to help cultivate that relationship with your dad, that takes a lot of strength, and I didn't want you to leave without me acknowledging that to you, friend to friend."

Jamal values building relationships with people. He often draws strength from them and vice versa. His grandma often talked to him about the importance of people and how they should be respected and loved at all times, no matter what. That concept isn't one that Jamal is always comfortable doing, but he knows that people are sometimes misled, and he believes in his heart that every human being wants to be loved and respected, so he makes sure he gives that at the highest level.

*****

Jamal finally receives a letter back from his dad after a couple of weeks, and in that letter, his dad provides him with his phone number so they could talk on the phone. Jamal saw the mailman drop off mail and for some reason he knew that letter would be there, it was on a Wednesday afternoon, sunny and not a cloud in the sky, when he woke up that morning a different feeling came over him, one he couldn't fully explain, but he knew it felt good.

He meditated, ate a good breakfast and said positive affirmation to himself as he walked to school. Saying things like, "you are amazing, you are worthy of greatness, you are greatness, your dad does love and miss you." He decided to change his mindset to things you wanted to happen or things that are already happening. That day just felt different, he said, and he felt so good, a feeling he will never forget. He is beginning to understand all of those things he and his god mom talked about months ago and how filling your thoughts with positivity can really change the way you see the world. He read that letter with so much joy and excitement, jumping up and down, reading it so loud that the neighbors could hear him. He found a pen and wrote that number down and couldn't wait to give him a call. In fact, he didn't want to waste any time before he called him, but he wanted to wait until his god mom got home before she called him.

As soon as she walked through the door, he ran to her and said, "guess what, guess what?! My dad wrote me back and gave me his phone number for me to call him. I'm about to speak to my dad!"

She gathers herself from his excitement and says, "it was only a matter of time, my son".

Jamal says, "I am about to call him right now. This should be an amazing conversation. We have so much to talk about."

His god mom says, "do you have some things you want to talk to him about in particular? If so, what is it?"

Jamal says, "you know what, I do have some things I would like to discuss with him, but I want the conversation to be organic and not scripted, so I am completely good with letting it flow, and if I am able to bring up certain things within the flow of the conversation, I am going to do just that."

His god mom responds and says, "I love that! Let me know how the conversation goes once you finish. I want to give you guys privacy, so you can really be able to engage with him and vice versa."

Jamal says, "alright, I am ready to give him a call and talk to him. This should be fun, and I am looking forward to just simply hearing his voice."

His god mom says, "yes, Jamal, it is the little things we must value and treasure, such as just being able to finally hear his voice."

Jamal gives his dad a call. The phone rings three times before he answers and says, "this is Curtis. How can I help you?"

Jamal smiles from ear to ear and says, "this is your son Jamal".

Curtis says, "wow! How are you, my son?! Thanks for calling me. When did you receive my letter? I sent it back as soon as I got yours."

Jamal says, "I am so happy to hear from you. It's been a long time coming. I am doing really good, I am so proud of myself, and I'll explain why as we continue to talk. I just got your letter today, and let me tell you, I was so happy that you responded back to me."

Curtis says, "I can't wait to hear about why you are proud of yourself and for you to explain it all to me. I also have some things I really want to talk to you about as well."

Jamal asks his dad, "do you know what trauma is?"

Curtis responds and says, "I definitely do."

Trauma is a deeply distressing or disturbing experience. Also, it is an emotional response to a terrible event like an accident, rape or natural disaster. Immediately after the event, shock and denial are typical. Longer-term reactions include unpredictable emotions, flashbacks, strained relationships and even physical symptoms like headaches or nausea. It seems like having trauma is a necessary uncomfortable thing to experience. In fact, there are three different types of traumas: acute, chronic and complex. Trauma can be handled in a number of different ways, seeking therapy to unlock some we may suppress, but first, you have to be willing to heal, make the conscious decision to do so, practice meditation, and accept support from loved ones. All of which are important and necessary to heal from whatever trauma you may experience.

Curtis hasn't been able to truly identify with that trauma mainly because he had not healed from it, despite thinking he may have been, but when he was talking to Jamal, he realized he wasn't fully healed and didn't know how to heal. Curtis is getting ready to unlock some of his past and do it in a way that will not only help him but help Jamal as well in his road to true forgiveness. Jamal is looking forward to his dad showing a level of vulnerability that he needs to see and that Curtis needs to portray; Jamal is a bit nervous because he doesn't know if his dad will be ready to bare it all emotionally.

Curtis was taught to "suck it up" and bury everything he experienced because that's what he thought a man did when in reality, men have to release certain things and discuss certain things so that when they get older, those things they suppressed as a child or teenager won't show up when they get older. Curtis just doesn't want Jamal to think that is how you deal with trauma. Luckily, Jamal understands that isn't the way to deal with it as well.

Jamal cherishes those therapy sessions with Dr. Sharice and is looking forward to talking to his dad about them. He wants to talk to him about what he learned, how to teach people how to treat him, how to forgive and let go, and most importantly, what it means to be one-hundred percent vulnerable. Healing is a process, and that process can't be self-mastered if one is in denial about what has caused them hurt and pain, whether it be emotionally or physically. Often times people can easily become in denial because not facing something that caused you to hurt or pain is looked at as easier to handle versus facing the situation head-on.

I challenge you all to go deep within yourself and ask yourself, "what pain and hurt have I suppressed?" How has that pain and hurt affected my relationships?" Once you discover that and truly tap into it and unlock those things, life becomes different, you become different, your perspective becomes different, and your evolution becomes inevitable. I am speaking from experience. Once all of those things began to happen, I started to view life differently, I started to value people more, and I started to really appreciate the conversations I would share with people and the conversations they would share with me. It takes a different mindset to allow yourself to relive certain pain but once you relive it can easily become dead if you allow it to.

A word that is associated with trauma is forgiveness. Forgiveness is a conscious, deliberate decision to release feelings of resentment or vengeance toward a person or group who has harmed you, regardless of whether they actually deserve your forgiveness. Jamal calls his dad and asks him, "who do you need to forgive, pops?"

Curtis says, "that is a great question, son, there are so many people I need to forgive, and it starts with my dad. I have never met him, he passed away six years ago due to health complications, and throughout that whole time when he was alive, he never reached out to me, and I began to grow resentment, and I didn't really realize that until he passed away."

Jamal says, "thanks for sharing that dad, I know that probably wasn't easy for you."

Curtis says, "I really needed to get that off of my chest. Thanks for encouraging me to discuss that. Life is often taken for granted, at least from my perspective. We always think our loved ones are going to be here physically when in reality, that is not the case. Although we all know that we still don't value our loved ones as much as we should, for whatever reasons."

Jamal says, "that is all very true, pops, and it is very unfortunate. People deal with a lot of hurt and pain, and often times it is caused by their loved ones. Instead of communicating and trying to find understanding, both people usually avoid one another so they don't have to address whatever the issue(s) might have been or might be. I want to live in a world where we aren't afraid to resolve conflict with our loved ones when we can voice our concerns to them about whatever it is or might be, and most importantly, communicate as soon as someone hurts you or does something that you don't approve of or appreciate."

Curtis responds and says, "great talk, son. I look forward to us having more conversations. Call me whenever and continue to strive for greatness."

*****

Jamal can't wait to talk to his god mom about the conversation he just had with his dad, but before he does so, he collects his thoughts and lays in his bed to do so. His god mom is excited for both of them; she knows and understands how much they both need each other moving forward and is determined to make sure they both understand that. Jamal walks out of his room and says, "we finally spoke. It felt great to hear from him. It has been a long time coming. We talked about so many different things, but us talking about forgiveness was really powerful. He talked about how his dad passed away and how he wasn't able to build a connection with him before he died. I could hear in his voice that that pain still affects him. We also talked about how growing up, he was taught to not show emotion or not have it, and in turn, he began to suppress all of his emotions because "that's not what men do". I didn't talk to him or question him about why he has been so absent in my life, but I definitely need answers to that question in particular."

She says, "well, I am glad you guys finally spoke after so much time has passed. I know that meant a lot to him as well. But I want to encourage you to ask all of the questions you need and want answers to, regardless of how you think it will make him feel. He should be uncomfortable answering certain questions, and it is nothing wrong with that. It is important for you to free yourself from the hurt and pain he has caused you emotionally, and he needs to know how he affected you. He needs to feel that hurt because that is the only way he can truly be a better father to you. You have to hold him accountable and be unapologetic about it."

Jamal says, "thank you for your words of wisdom. I will make sure to hold him accountable and be unapologetic about expressing my feelings." Jamal has one final question for his god mom, "what is the best way to resolve conflict? In your opinion."

She said, "I love that question. I think the best way to resolve any conflict is to express how you truly feel, don't try to spare the other person's feelings, try to do it in person and not over the phone or through text, maintain eye contact with the person or people involved, really speak from your heart, discuss why they hurt you and what you would've preferred from them. I could go on and on, but I think those are great starting points to having that conversation with someone. You got this I know it seems like a lot and it is, but it is all necessary for you to heal from the pain he has caused you."

Jamal says, "you are right, I am confident that I will be able to have this conversation and I am also confident that my dad and I will have a great relationship moving forward."

Chapter Sixteen

As their sophomore year is coming to an end, Jamal and Sabrina wanted to meet with their counselor again to see what type of progress has been made with their idea of having classes that help students and teachers with their anxiety, depression and their social skills. He lets them know that great progress has been made and that it is very likely the campus will see classes that will help both students and teachers next school year so that way it can get the proper rollout. He also asks Jamal if he would be cool with being the president of these clubs because they will have to be electives because they can't force students and parents to take part in those electives. Parents would have to sign waivers in order for their students to take part in the class.

Jamal says, "I would love to be the president. I would also love if Sabrina could be my vice president because she has great ideas and really has a good understanding of what emotional support can look like for our school moving forward. Sabrina, would you like to be the vice president?"

Sabrina says, "of course, I would love that!"

Their junior year had the making of being monumental and ground-breaking, and they had no idea what kind of greatness was on the horizon. But before their sophomore year was over, both Jamal and Sabrina still had one thing to do before they could say the year was a true success, and that was letting the students and staff know about what would be available for the next year, but they had to figure out a way that was cool and fun. They decided to market it and promote it throughout the neighborhood with posters, fundraisers, social media and last but not least, word of mouth.

Before you knew it, it was circulating throughout social media, and other schools would begin to look into it and ask questions. Jamal being the spokesperson, took a lot of pride in not only answering questions but also encouraging other school leaders to come to see it all in action when the next school year rolled around. They were able to raise close to $50,000 for various supplies, guest speakers, and even incentives for teachers to want to participate or lead discussions because Jamal knew to get buy-in from staff, he had to ultimately fund them, and he had no problem doing that.

Neither Jamal nor Sabrina received much feedback from the staff, but they both remained hopeful and then decided to host an open house at the school and only wanted to invite staff to hear any protentional issues they may have and to just get overall feedback. Jamal wanted to make sure several teachers and staff were in attendance because he knew the value they would bring and also how much the students appreciated those several staff members. Fortunately, he was able to get all those to attend and right before the event started, he began to notice the hashtag on social media #INTHECLASSROOMWECUREANXIETY. So, of course, he wanted to make this a huge deal and rightfully so. The power of social media is one that can't be denied, and if you can gain any traction for a cause, it is in your best interest to take full advantage and not let that momentum die down or fade.

*****

On another note, there has been something that has been on Jamal's mind for some time now, and that was asking Sabrina out on a date. They have been to the homecoming dance before, but Jamal doesn't view that as a traditional date, which I can agree with. Jamal wanted to get some advice from his god mom about how to ask her, where to take her, and should he ask permission from her parents. All of this was new to him. All he knew was he wanted to spend time with her in a different setting than normal and wanted her to feel appreciated and valued as not only his friend but someone he was interested in on a romantic level.

First, he asked his god mom, "can I talk to you about something?"

She said, "of course, you can. What is on your mind?"

Jamal says, "I want to ask Sabrina out on a date, but I don't know how."

She says, "that's great! You have come to the right person", as she smiles.

Jamal says, "how should I approach the situation, do I just come right out and ask?"

She says, "yes, I don't think you should overthink it at all. As a matter of a fact, she may be waiting for you to ask her, and she will be just as nervous and excited as you are, which is a good thing. I recommend asking her in person, not over the phone or through text."

Jamal says, "thank you so much! I will ask her in person, and I look forward to her response regardless of how nervous I will be."

His god mom says, "go for it sooner than later, no need to wait another week, please let me know how it goes. You have my full support."

Jamal says, "I look forward to doing this", as he smiles nervously. "I just hope her parents allow this to happen, which I don't know if they will."

Jamal leaves his god mom room and begins to come up with a plan on how he wants to ask Sabrina out on a date. He had several ideas, but ultimately, he decided to keep it simple and as her while they walked to the park to hang out. But before all of that could happen, he needed to ask her to go with him to the park, this isn't something they normally did, but he thought this was a great way to talk to her about wanting to take her out on a date.

So, he gave her a call, "Sabrina, what's up! I miss you; do you have any plans tomorrow?"

Sabrina says, "Jamal, I was just thinking about you, and I miss you too. No, I don't have any plans tomorrow; what's up?"

Jamal says, "I was wondering if you would like to go to the park with me tomorrow and spend some time together."

Sabrina says, "I would love to; what time did you want to go?"

Jamal says, "great! Let's go at 2 pm."

Sabrina says, "sounds good to me".

Jamal quickly began to notice that he doesn't know much about Sabrina in regard to what she likes to eat and other hobbies she might enjoy. Sabrina wastes no time asking her mom if she could go on a date with Jamal. Sabrina runs into her mom's room and says, "mom, mom, Jamal asked me out on a date, and it would be our first one! I am so excited; I am not sure what to do with all of my excitement" as she smiles and gives her mom a hug.

Connie says, "this would be you guys' first date?! It seems like you guys have been on multiple dates already, but I guess not. I am excited for both of you. Where is he going to take you?"

Sabrina says, "yea, I know! But this is our first date, and hopefully, many more to come. We are going to go to the park tomorrow at 2 pm; I am so nervous.

Connie says, "that sounds like a lot of fun! It is perfectly ok to be nervous. I am sure he is just as nervous, if not more nervous than you are. My advice would be just having fun. You guys are already good friends, so that will work in both of you guys' favor. There's a certain level of comfort that is already there naturally, which is a really big deal."

Sabrina says, "thanks mom, I appreciate you saying all of those things. It helps me put things into their proper perspective. Do you think dad will have a problem with me going on a date with Jamal?"

Connie says, "not at all. Just give him a call and let him know. I am sure he will be just as supportive as I am."

Now Sabrina has a different level of confidence, knowing her mom and dad support her in going on a date with Jamal. Now all she has to do is find something to wear, which can be a task, especially when going on a first date. She asks her mom what she should wear because she tried on several outfits and couldn't decide which one to wear.

Connie says, "you should wear some blue denim jeans with a long sleeve crop top. Keep it simple and comfortable."

Sabrina says, "I love that idea mom I was trying on dresses and other things, and it just wasn't coming together, but I think your idea of denim with a long sleeve crop top would be perfect."

Sabrina asks, "do you think I should ask Jamal what he is

going to wear? Or do you think that would be weird?"

Connie says, "you can ask him, but I think you should just play it cool. He will be more than ready for this, and you will see. You guys might dress the same minus the crop top, of course. But you can never go wrong with blue denim jeans" as she shrugs her shoulders.

Sabrina asks her mom, "what should I expect on my first date?"

Connie says, "that is a great question. I would say, expect to have fun, enjoy some great conversation, to be nervous, which you have already pointed out. I'll share my experience with you about my first date. We went to the movies; he was such a gentleman. He made sure I was comfortable, he was very complimentary, and overall, he was awesome. He asked me by writing me a note and sliding it into my locker in high school. We were in the 9th grade. He was really an amazing young man. Unfortunately, he was shot two times and killed while walking home from school."

Sabrina says, "oh wow, mom, I didn't think that would be the end of that story; that is so tough and hard to hear. I know that was hard for you to experience. But I am glad you both got a chance to enjoy one another as long as you both could. How are you? I know reliving that wasn't easy at all. But I really appreciate you telling me that."

Connie says, "I am doing good; thanks for asking me that question. It gave me a real chance to reminisce on the past and let some emotion out. I needed that more than I thought I did, but I wanted to kind of let you know what to expect if Jamal really likes you like I think he does."

Sabrina smiles awkwardly and laughs, "mom, but I have one

more question, and I hope I don't get in trouble, did…. you guys kiss?"

Connie says, "you won't get in trouble for asking me that. In fact, I am glad you did. It lets me know you feel safe with asking me questions like that, and I completely understand, I was once a sixteen-year-old girl, so I completely get it. To answer your question, we did kiss, but keep in mind he was a complete gentleman and didn't force me at all. It was something I wanted to do, and so we did it. He didn't try to make me feel bad even if I didn't want to, he was so supportive, and I will always appreciate him for that."

Sabrina says, "thank you for sharing that with me, mom. It means so much to me that you were able to put yourself in my shoes. The reason I thought you were going to get mad at me is because of how young we are and how it could lead to other things like having sex."

Connie says, "you are right! It could lead to other things and what I will say is that you always have to be conscious about every decision you make especially when it comes to having any type of sexual relations with the opposite sex. The bond you guys have created could make you feel like it is something you have to do, but you definitely don't, and I would advise you to either. You have many years ahead of you before you need to think about losing your virginity. I am so glad that you want to have this conversation, though, it is one I have been putting off for years because I was scared, and I didn't know how I would handle the conversation. No one had a talk with me about my virginity and how important it was to keep it. Because once you lose it, you cannot get it back. I recommend holding on to it; trust me, you will be glad you did."

Sabrina says, "thanks, mom, for being understanding. I am glad we can have an open dialogue like this, you have been so open with me about this topic, and it really gives me some clarity and insight on what I should do and how I should go about it. I have every intention of waiting to lose my virginity, and I say that with all of the confidence in the world. I feel really good about taking my time and also explaining that to anybody I will be interested in, that will have to respect that and if not, then they won't be someone I need to waste my time with. I have learned so much from your mom, not just by the things you say but also by the things you don't necessarily say. You are my hero, mom, and you deserve everything in this world that you desire. I love you!"

As Connie's eyes begin to water, she says, "you are truly an amazing young woman, and as much as I would want to take the credit for that, I know I can't. Thank you for being you, Sabrina. You are a true inspiration!"

Sabrina smiles and says, "what a great talk, mom! I have no idea of the depths this conversation would take us."

*****

Now it was time for Sabrina to tell her dad about her date and also the conversation she had with her mom. But first, she wanted to talk to her mom about how she should approach the conversation with her dad.

Connie says, "just approach it the same way you did with me. Upfront and honest, your dad would really appreciate that. You should even talk to him about the conversation we had about losing your virginity and kissing. It's going to be tough for him to hear, but he should hear it from you, and of course, I will be right here to support you. So, Sabrina decides not to waste any more time giving her dad a call.

He answers with so much excitement, "hello my little angel, how's everything going?"

Sabrina says, "everything is going great dad, thanks for asking. It is something I wanted to talk to you about, but I am really nervous to tell you."

Keith says, "what's on your mind? I am here for you."

Sabrina says, "well, Jamal asked me out on a date to the park tomorrow at 2 pm, and I really want to go. I already spoke to mom about it, and she was extremely supportive, so much so that we had a very detailed conversation, one that was really necessary."

Keith says, "this is exciting! I am glad you and your mom had a great conversation about it, and you feel encouraged. Your mom has really great insight, and I am sure she gave you some great advice. I also want to give you some advice, but first, I want to let you know I fully support you going on a date with Jamal. I think he is a great young man, and I also see how much you guys enjoy one another. My advice to you would be to have fun, require him to be a gentleman, and don't be afraid to say no, especially if it is something you don't want to do."

Sabrina says, "thanks, dad! I really appreciate your support and the advice you gave as well. You and mom had similar advice, which is pretty cool. I did talk to mom about kissing, and we also talked about virginity. I wanted to let you know because you deserve to know."

Keith says, "I am sure your mom did a great job discussing those things with you, I know this is around the time where you start to think about those things, and I am glad you felt comfortable enough to discuss it instead of just going to do those things. I am so proud of you, and you are an amazing young woman. Thank you for trusting me with that information and for being vulnerable.

Sabrina says, "wow, you aren't mad or anything, dad?"

Keith says, "no, not at all. I admire you for voicing your concerns and just asking questions. I know that wasn't easy for you to do, and you should be commended for that. Where's your mom?"

Connie yells, "I am right here" she says with a big smile on her face.

Keith says, "our baby girl is growing up, isn't she?"

Connie says, "that is very true, and I can't wait to continue to see her grow and develop into the woman she will be."

Chapter Seventeen

The next day has arrived, which is the day for Jamal and Sabrina to go on their first date. It is a beautiful day. The sun is beaming and not a cloud in the sky, and seventy-five degrees outside. Jamal called Sabrina as soon as he woke up, which was at 8 am. Sabrina was still asleep but definitely called him back as soon as she woke up, which was at 9 am. During 8 am and 9 am, for the one-hour, Jamal got his outfit ready, cleaned his shoes, he even took a walk to the park just to scope out where they would hang out. He wanted to have somewhat of a plan.

As he was walking back home, he remembered Sabrina saying she loved picnics and always thought they were so cute. So, naturally, Jamal made sandwiches and asked his god mom to get some fruit. He wanted her to get strawberries, grapes, cherries, and watermelon. All of which he and Sabrina both enjoy. Sabrina calls him back. Jamal answers and says, "Sabrina, what is up? Good morning, it is such a beautiful for our date. Go look outside and see for yourself. I have such a cool date planned for us. I can't wait. I will give you another call once I am on my way to come to pick you up. See you later, Sabrina."

Sabrina says, "yes, you are right! It is a great day. I am looking forward to seeing what you have planned for us, I know you have put a lot of thought into it, and I am so appreciative. I will see you later."

*****

Jamal had a few more hours before he went to go pick up Sabrina. He wanted to call his dad again, mainly because of his excitement but also because he wanted to talk to him about the time he took his mom out on a date. Jamal was extremely hesitant to ask his dad because he wasn't sure if his dad would want to talk about it. Jamal swallowed his pride and gave his dad a call, "what's up, dad! I have a few more hours before I pick up Sabrina for our date at the park. I wanted to ask you a question."

Curtis is excited and says, "what's up, son! What's on your mind?"

Jamal says, "well, I wanted to ask you about the time you took my mom on a date, and I wanted to know how it went. I don't want to make you uncomfortable, but I never really had a chance to talk to you about anything about her, and I was hoping right now would be a great time."

Curtis says, "wow, I would be honored to talk to you about the first time I took your mom on a date. In fact, anytime you have a question about her or anything, just let me know, and I will do my best to answer it as best as I can. I took her to a restaurant that was no longer open. It was a popular milk shake spot that a lot of teenagers went to on Friday and Saturday nights. I had been planning to take her there for at least a month, but I was too scared to ask her. But finally, I said to myself, what is the worst that could happen. So, I walked up to her in between classes and said, "what are you doing this Friday night?" She said, "nothing at all. I don't have any plans. Why, what's up?" I said, "I would love to take you to get a milk shake. Is that cool with you?" She said, "I love milk shakes, that sounds good to me." Once we got to the milk shake place everything was so perfect, to be honest, it was like we had known each other for years and years. But I had only known her for about five months. I transferred to her high school from a previous high school in the middle of my freshman year. As soon as I saw her, I knew I wanted to be more than friends with her. I was able to spend so much time with her; she was really my best friend, she knew me just as well as I knew her. She was really a blessing to me and so many other people. Her presence was liberating, and when she entered a room, you knew she was there. I hope I'm doing a good job of explaining how awesome she was, and not a day goes by when I don't think about her in some way, shape or form. I am always honored whenever I get a chance to talk about her, and I am even more honored I get to talk to our only child about her. I apologize for not being forthcoming with information about her. I will do a better job of mentioning her because I know it will mean a lot to you, and it will also make me feel good.

Jamal says, "well said, dad, well said, that was great! You had me captivated, and I didn't want you to stop talking about her and you guys' experiences. That was truly inspiring. I feel much more comfortable going on my date. It seems like you guys were able to just relax and appreciate each other's company, which I fully intend on being able to do with Sabrina. You can look forward to hearing from me tomorrow morning or afternoon, so I can tell you all about my date."

Curtis says, "it was my pleasure, son, and of course! I look forward to hearing all about it. Have fun and remember to enjoy her and let her enjoy you; you will be just fine." Jamal says, "alright, dad! Talk to you later!"

*****

The time has finally come for Jamal to get ready for his date; he sets his clothes out on his bed, like what he would do for his first day of school after a long summer break. But this time, the circumstances were a lot different. He had his first date with Sabrina. Joyce knocks on his door to make sure he isn't going to be late and says, "Jamal, Jamal, are you getting ready?" No response from Jamal because he had already jumped into the shower. Joyce realized he was in the shower and walked back to her room with a pleasant smile on her face.

Jamal took a quick fifteen-minute shower, brushed his teeth, and then put his clothes on. By this time, it was 1:08, and their date was at 2 pm, so he had time to prep himself in the mirror for about ten minutes, so he did just that. For the first minute or so, he had a hard time taking himself seriously. I mean, he was talking to himself, acting like he was talking to Sabrina. You could imagine how funny that might be. Once he settled in and got all of his jitters out, he got really serious and focused on his energy and delivery.

Joyce overheard him talking to himself from her room, so she knocked on his door and asked if she could come in. Jamal's eyes got big, and he didn't want to say anything because he was embarrassed. He realized his god mom had heard him talking to himself. She came in and said, "you don't want to overthink this son. You will do just fine. I commend you for wanting to practice but remember she is one of your good friends, and this is her first date too. It is such thing as being overprepared because you could easily get in your head and overanalyze this date."

Jamal says, "what does overanalyze mean?"

Joyce says, "it means to analyze something in great detail."

Jamal says, "that is exactly what I am doing. I should get going. I have a picnic for us, sandwiches and some of her favorite fruit. I am going to put it all in my backpack and head to her house."

Joyce says, "that is great. She will really appreciate that! Have fun, and remember you got this! I love you, son!"

Jamal yells, "I love you too, god mom." Jamal calls Sabrina to let her know he is on his way. "What's up, Sabrina, I just wanted to let you know I was leaving my house now and on my way to come to pick you up."

Sabrina says, "ok, I will be ready when you get here. I can't wait to see you."

Jamal smiles and says, "we are about to have a lot of fun."

*****

Jamal is finally headed to Sabrina's house. While walking to pick her up, he thinks about ways to impress her. But as soon as he starts to do that, he thinks back on the conversations he had with his dad and his god mom and how they encouraged him to not over-analyze this date. He thinks about how he's going to ask her for a kiss and when he's going to do it. So many thoughts are going through his head, and he is so nervous despite everyone telling him he shouldn't be. He just wants to make sure Sabrina knows how he feels about her, he also wants to make sure he knows how Sabrina feels about him. Because as of now, they just have a very close friendship, but he would like it to be more, much more. He regrets not asking his dad or

God mom how to ask Sabrina how to be his girlfriend, but he makes sure he has the thoughts for the outcome he wants, which was some advice he learned from Dr. Sharice, how our thoughts become things.

Jamal walks up to the door and knocks three times. Connie answers the door and says, "hello Jamal, it is so good to see you. Sabrina will be out in about 10 minutes; she's changing her outfit."

Jamal says, "hello Ms. Connie, it is so good to see you as well. No worries, I am in no rush. She can take as much time as she needs. I thought about changing my outfit too, but I decided not to."

Connie says, "you look great! I like the outfit you chose; I am glad you are being patient with her. Sometimes outfits we have in our mind look great, but once we put them on, it is a different story, then the outfits we don't think we look good end up looking great" as she laughs.

Jamal had been waiting for fifteen minutes, and then Sabrina finally came out of her room. Jamal stopped mid-sentence while talking to her mom and could not take his eyes off her. He says, "Sabrina, you look amazing."

Sabrina returns a compliment back to him and says, "thank you! You look good too!"

Jamal asks, "are you ready to go on our date?"

Sabrina says, "I definitely am. I will see you later, mom."

Jamal says, "I will have her back home by 6 pm Ms. Connie, right before it gets dark."

Ms. Connie says, "that works for me, have a great time, guys and be safe."

Jamal and Sabrina leave the house and begin walking to the park. Both are nervous and shy, so neither one of them says anything to one other for about five minutes. Jamal was thinking, "I hope she likes what I have planned for her", he even thought to tell her because he didn't know how she would respond to the surprise. Sabrina was thinking, "I can't believe we are finally on a date; it seems to be just as excited as me, but I don't know if I should ask him."

Jamal breaks the ice and asks her, "how was your day?"

Sabrina says, "I had a good day, despite changing my outfit a few times" as she laughs. "How was your day," she says.

Jamal says, "I had a really good day, I was nervous, and to be honest, I am still nervous, but it is a good thing."

Sabrina says, "I have those same feelings, a lot of nerves, but I think it is me being more excited than nervous."

Jamal says, "yes, that makes a lot of sense. I had wanted to ask you on a date, but I was scared. To be honest, I wasn't one-hundred percent sure you would say yes."

Sabrina says, "wow! Really, I was hoping you would ask me," as she smiles. "I am glad you did. There was no way I was going to say no to you asking me out on a date."

Jamal says, "I am definitely glad the feeling was mutual. I talked myself out of asking you out so many times. You have no idea."

Sabrina says, "well, we are here now, and I am so glad."

As they are approaching the park, Sabrina notices the picnic set-up Jamal had worked on. She looks at him and says, "Wow, this looks amazing, Jamal; who helped you?"

Jamal says, "thank you! I really wanted to make this day as special for us as I possibly could. You mean a lot to me, and I wanted to show you that you do."

Sabrina says, "you mean a lot to me too! I am glad that feeling is mutual as well. Sometimes I only thought you liked me as a friend and nothing else."

Jamal says, "it is interesting how we both thought the same things about one another, and we were completely off", as he laughs out loud. Jamal says, "let's make our way to the picnic area I have for us. I made some sandwiches and got some of your favorite fruit."

She smiles and says, "this is so beautiful, thank you so much! I knew you were up to something when you asked me what my favorite fruit was, but I had no idea it was this. You really must like me," she says sarcastically with a slight grin on her face, and then she whispers under her breath I really like you too. But Jamal was too far away, so he didn't hear her.

Jamal was in the process of making a plate for her, but she stopped him and said, "I'll make your plate for you; you can sit down and relax."

Sabrina recalls seeing her mom always make plates for her dad, and so she wanted to adopt that same philosophy when it came to Jamal. Jamal was taking a back because he wasn't used to receiving that kind of treatment on any level, nor has he seen it take place. As the two enjoyed their lunch, Jamal couldn't help but to keep looking at her, not just because she was beautiful to him but because he really appreciated her for who she was. The two continued to have conversations about their futures, mainly independently, but Jamal wanted to make sure she knew he wanted to be more than friends, so he decided to finally tell her in detail how he felt about her, in hopes those feelings would be received mutually, after all, prior to him wanting to bring this up, they have had talks of liking one another past just a friendship.

Jamal says, "I really like our vibe. It's pretty damn cool. I wanted to take you out on a date not just because I wanted to spend time with you in a different environment but also because I wanted to let you know how I really feel about you and those feelings go past us just being friends. I see so much more with you, and I want so much more with you. Sabrina, I would love to be your boyfriend, how do you feel about that?"

Sabrina's eyes got big, and she says, "thank you for those kind words, you really mean a lot to me too. I was waiting for you to ask me this great question, I've even practiced how I would answer it in the mirror" as she laughs out loud. "I would love to be your girlfriend, I have always saw you as more than just a friend, when I say always, I mean ALWAYS. I just wasn't one-hundred percent sure if you wanted the same thing, but now I know you did, and I am so happy. I can't wait to tell my mom and dad."

Jamal says, "I am so happy right now" as he stands up and reaches his hands out to Sabrina so he can give her a hug. As soon as he went in for a hug he kissed her on her lips. Sabrina reciprocated the kiss and began kissing him back. She was surprised he did it, but boy was she happy he did. She's thought about this day for such a long time, and to see it come to fruition she was excited beyond words. Once the two finished their kiss, they looked at each other and laughed. The laugh was full of joy and excitement.

The two spent about three hours at the park. Jamal looks at his watch and says, "I think it's time for me to walk you back home."

Sabrina says, "I agree. Let's not give our parents any reason to be worried or overly concerned about how long we've been gone. My mom would be expecting me soon anyway, so good call Jamal."

Jamal says, "you're right! My god mom will be expecting me soon too. I really enjoyed you today, Sabrina."

Sabrina says, "I really enjoyed you as well. We have to do this more often. How do you feel about that?"

Jamal says, "I'm glad the feeling is mutual. Yes, we do have to do this more often and we will."

Jamal walks Sabrina back home safely. Sabrina knocks on her door and waits for her mom to open it. Connie says, "welcome back from your date. I can't wait to hear all about it. Jamal, thank you for protecting my daughter and taking good care of her", she says with a huge smile on her face.

Jamal says, "it was my pleasure, Sabrina is amazing, and I am thankful to have her in my life. Thank you for trusting me, it really means a lot to me."

Connie says, "of course! You are an amazing young man, and I am thankful for you as well. You should hurry and get home before it gets dark. I know your god mom is patiently awaiting your return home."

Jamal says, "thank you, Ms. Connie! You are right about that. I will see you guys later." But before he left, he had to give Sabrina a hug, and he did just that. While her mom looked and them and smiled. Jamal leaves Sabrina's house and gives his god mom a call to let her know he is on his way home. "I am on my way home; I had a great time with Sabrina. I can't wait to tell you all about it. Joyce says, "thank you for calling me and letting me know. I am looking forward to hearing all about it! I can tell by the excitement in your voice that you and Sabrina had a great time. I didn't expect anything less than that." Jamal says, "I will see you soon!"

Jamal gets back home and is greeted by Joyce with a warm hug and a huge smile. She says, "sit down, sit down. Tell me all about it."

Jamal says, "well, when we got there, she saw the picnic and all of her favorite fruit. She was happy, we sat down, began eating and talking. I told her how I felt about her, which is us me wanting to be more than just friends with her." Boy, oh boy, was I nervous, but luckily, she felt the same exact way. She said she had been waiting on me to express interest in her that would surpass just our friendship. I'm glad I told her how I felt. It was all worth it, despite me being scared and nervous. I stepped outside of my comfort zone, and it paid off. I was so proud of myself."

Joyce says, "wow! Jamal, that is amazing, I am glad you went for it and didn't hold back. You guys deserve the absolute best, and it looks like you guys are in route to making sure you guys get what you deserve, and I am proud of both of you."

Jamal says, "but, wait. I have more to share with you." Joyce's eyes get big, and she says, "what else?"

Jamal says, "I also asked her to be my girlfriend, and she said yes! She said yes without hesitation. It was like she was waiting for me to ask for a while now."

Joyce says, "wow! I didn't expect you to say that at all! I am not surprised at all, though. You guys have a great friendship and bond. Does her parents know yet?"

Jamal says, "wait, one more thing, we also kissed!"

Joyce says, "that is amazing! I am sure you were a complete gentleman and didn't force her to do anything she didn't want to do. I didn't think you would even try, but I am glad you did what you wanted to do in the moment."

Jamal says, "yea, it was all very nerve-wracking, but all in all, I am glad I went for it. And I did not pressure her at all. We hugged, and then I leaned in for a kiss, and she leaned in as well."

Joyce says, "do you think her parents are going to be supportive of everything?"

Jamal says, "that is a great question; what I do know is this. Sabrina and I talked about having open and honest conversations with our parents about our date; she said she would let her mom and dad know everything. To answer your question, yes! I do think they will be one-hundred percent supportive."

Joyce says, "last question, are you going to let your dad know about your date? I know he was looking forward to hearing about it."

Jamal says, "I am definitely going to call him and let him know. As a matter of a fact, I am going to call him now."

Jamal walks to his room, calls his dad, the phone rings two times and then his dad answers, "what's up, son! How's it going?

Jamal says, "everything is going well. I wanted to let you know how great my date was. We kissed, and I asked her to be my girlfriend and she happily accepted."

Curtis says, "wow! Straight to the point uh, son," as he laughs. I am glad you stepped outside of your comfort zone. It seems like it was well worth it."

*****

Sabrina calls her dad and puts him on speaker; she wanted to tell both parents about her date; mom and dad, "I want to talk to you guys about my date. It was great! From the beginning to the end. Jamal was a complete gentleman and made sure I was comfortable the entire time. I should've taken pictures so I could show you guys; we had a picnic at the park, with some of our favorite fruit and sandwiches. I will check and see if Jamal took pictures, I am hoping he did. We shared a great conversation, and it was never a dull or weird moment between the two of us and I was surprised that it wasn't to be honest. We talked about everything from our friendship to making it more than that to even sharing a passionate kiss."

Once she mentioned them sharing a passionate kiss, she thought her mom or dad would interrupt her, but they did not. So, she continued to talk to her parents about her dad and proceeded to mention how Jamal expressed his feelings towards her beyond just a friendship and how she was taken aback but ultimately felt the same way, and from there, the two talked about being in a relationship. That's when her dad interjected and began to express his level of happiness and excitement for her and Jamal.

He said, "that is amazing, Sabrina! I am glad he treated you with respect and kindness. Honestly, I didn't expect him to do nothing less than that. Seems like the nerves for you guys quickly vanished, which is commendable, and I contribute that to you guys friendship and bond. It is strong, and I don't think either one of you really recognized it because you guys are in it, but I believe people on the outside can see how strong it is. Your mom, me, his god mom and even his dad, even though he hasn't physically seen you guys in action like we have. I am happy for you both, and I look forward to you guys having many more great moments and being able to continue sharing them with one another."

Connie adds, "well said, dad, I couldn't have said it better myself. I am genuinely proud of you and happy for you. Jamal is a great young man, and you are a great young woman. Thank for being honest with us about what you guys did, I know that wasn't the easiest thing to do, but you said it all with grace and love."

Sabrina says, "thanks, mom and dad! You both have instilled a level of confidence in me that is hard for me to explain, but you guys always make me feel empowered when I discuss certain topics, and this is no different. I am a very lucky daughter to have you guys as parents, and I don't take it for granted. You guys really make me feel comfortable talking to you about any and everything. When Jamal told me, he wanted to be more than friends, I was surprised and happy at the same time. Mainly because I didn't see that coming at all. After he told me that, I made sure to let him know how I felt about him just as well, I told him how I not only appreciated our friendship but how I always saw us being more, and he just smiled and nodded his head. I enjoyed everything about our date. Literally everything, we even talked about making sure we tell our guardians, and of course, he was nervous about me telling you guys all of this, but I assure him you guys would be extremely supportive and you guys have been just that."

Keith says, "my daughter, my daughter, what an amazing experience, and I am glad you got to share it when a young man like Jamal. Have you guys discussed when you are going to have your next date? Or are you guys mainly focused on the next school year, which will be here in no time."

Sabrina says, "we haven't discussed when and where our next date will be, but I was thinking I would initiate it and plan it. As far as the next school year, I am excited to be a junior, and I know Jamal is too. The school should be implementing classes to help students with stress and anxiety, as well as for the teachers. I am extremely excited about that. School can be overwhelming, from testing, socially, getting accepted to colleges, just to name a few things."

Chapter Eighteen

Jamal and Sabrina get ready for their junior year of high school; they both already know what classes they want to take and which teachers they want to have. Neither one knows if they want to attend a four-year university but they both know they don't want to work for anyone, and they want to own their own business. Sabrina realized early on that she wanted to own her own business because she had the pleasure of watching her mom, and she began to see what it took to not only own her own business but also how important it is to hire people who you can trust with your vision.

For Jamal, his inspiration for wanting his own business comes from one of his idols, Earvin "Magic" Johnson, the hall of fame point guard for the Los Angeles Lakers, he has studied how Magic grew his business before he retired from the National Basketball Association (NBA). Jamal's love for real estate is growing rapidly, so much so, he wants to encourage his current high school to teach more kids about it, and he feels he can be successful being able to encourage a curriculum for it. Jamal was so encouraged by his thoughts, that he wanted to act on them. By doing so he sent his counselor an email and asked if he could have a meeting with him on the first day of school.

Jamal was thinking he could talk to him about real estate and hopefully he could have some type of class that teaches his peers and other staff, like his approach with the class about handling stress, anxiety and other obstacles he and other students may be faced with. He mentioned this Sabrina as well, and a few other classmates, and they all agreed with this idea. The only issue Jamal and his classmates might run into is getting another innovative approved.

Jamal is extremely optimistic because he and the others just want to see things improve and evolve from the normal way school has been for the past fifty-plus years. Sabrina has an idea on how they could make this happens sooner than later, she decides to start a petition, and she plans to have former students, current students, former staff and current staff sign it. She thinks this could be the start of having what they want at their school for years to come even once they graduate. The current school model is one that is dated and needs to improve for multiple reasons that Sabrina doesn't care to explain or get into. Most staff agree that the school curriculum needs to change but they just don't have the energy nor want to give the correct amount of effort to improve it. But have no worries, Jamal and Sabrina are there to rescue everyone.

On their first day of school, Jamal and Sabrina walked into their counselor's office to notice he wasn't there. Not only was he not there, but he would also no longer be at the school because he had moved to Georgia. Neither Sabrina nor Jamal knew that would be happening so they both looked at one another, confused and shocked. Their new counselor was named Timothy Justice, who had been a college counselor for ten years prior to coming to support this high school. At least their previous counselor alerted Mr. Justice about everything, and he was aware of why they were coming to the office.

He said, "you guys must be Jamal and Sabrina, your previous counselor spoke so highly of both of you. Rest assured I believe in what you guys are trying to do, and I appreciate you guys for doing it. You have my full support, and I will make sure we get both initiatives up and running within the next two to three months, hopefully, sooner."

Jamal says, "it is nice to meet you Mr. Justice. Thank you for your support. I believe with your help we will be able to make this a better school for the present students and staff and the future students and staff."

Sabrina says, "I am slightly confused but nonetheless glad to have you a part of our school. You seem like an awesome man who brings tons of experience."

Mr. Justice says, "thanks, young people, this is going to be an amazing year, and I can't wait to be introduced to your classmates, I know they'll be shocked but trust me when I say, I love what I do, and I love serving the youth."

When Jamal gets his class schedule, he notices that Mr. Justice teaches a leadership class and that he is in it. Jamal didn't know how to feel about it, but he could say he was more excited than not. So much so, that he called Sabrina and asked her about her schedule, and she let him know that she was also in that class. Neither one of them knew what to expect, but both were excited to be a part of a class that was new to their school.

Jamal walked back to Mr. Justice's office to ask him about the class and why he was in it, and Mr. Justice said, "you will see what the class is about in sixth period along with your peers. It is fifteen students who are in the class who have been identified as leaders at the school from ninth to twelfth graders."

*****

A new student by the name of Sonya Gillespie enrolled in their school; she moved from Arizona. She was in Jamal's Math and English class. She was immediately impressed with how he carried himself and quickly noticed how different he was from the guys back where she was from. She sat next to him in their English class and made sure she introduced herself, "hi Jamal, my name is Sonya. Nice to meet you."

Jamal says, "hello, Sonya, nice to meet you too. Did you go here last year? If so, I don't remember seeing you."

Sonya says, "no, I am from Arizona, Phoenix to be exact. This is my first year here, and I like it so far. It is much different from my high school in Arizona. At my old high school, it seemed like the teachers were just getting a paycheck, and they weren't really invested in our education or our future. But here, it seems as if the teachers care, and they value each student. So much so, Mr. Justice has a leadership class, and he placed me in it. I am excited to see what that class is about."

Jamal says, "wow, I couldn't imagine being at a school where the teachers didn't care. Welcome to our school, I am glad you are having a much better experience here, and it is only day one. That is interesting, Mr. Justice also placed me and my girlfriend in that class too. Along with other students from all four grade levels."

Sonya says, "thank you for welcoming me; you said you have a girlfriend? That's awesome! How long have you guys been together?"

Jamal says, "I definitely do have a girlfriend. Her and I have been knowing each other since seventh grade and have been friends since that time. During this past summer, I finally asked her to be my girlfriend, and she accepted. I was so nervous to ask her because I didn't know what her response would be, but fortunately, she felt the same way, and we have been enjoying one another outside of just our friendship since. I love telling that story, it makes me feel amazing, every time."

Sonya says, "that is an amazing story and one that I appreciate. I am glad you found someone that makes you feel great. I had a boyfriend back home, but we decided to break up because of the long distance and how difficult that would be for the both of us. I kind of wish I didn't agree to that, but what's done is done. I truly want what the best for him, regardless of if it is with me or not. He is an amazing person and someone I am glad I got a chance to not only get to know but to learn from as well."

Jamal says, "I appreciate that level of maturity. I am sure he wishes the same for you, and who knows, maybe once you guys get older and more mature, you guys can reconnect on that level. I am going to meet up with my girlfriend right now. I will see you later in leadership class."

*****

Jamal meets up with Sabrina, and they discuss their first day of school to that point. They both are excited about their junior year, they are both looking forward to their leadership class, and they love how new and fresh it feels. Jamal lets her know about Sonya and how could she seem to be.

Jamal says, "I have a new student in my math class named Sonya, she's from Arizona. We had a very cool conversation; she is also in our leadership class. I think you guys will get a long well."

Sabrina says, "that's pretty cool! I am glad you have someone in your class that you bond with. I am looking forward to meeting her later today."

Sabrina is at a point where she loves high school but doesn't know if she wants to attend college. She's struggling with how to mention that to her parents, but if she knows one thing, she knows her parents are supportive and have proven to be all her life. She was walking through the hallways and noticed all the college banners and former alumni who attend those schools. She scheduled a meeting with Mr. Justice; although she doesn't know him that well, she feels like she can have a conversation with him about it, and she trusts his judgement and opinion. The pressure and anxiety are overwhelming; she knows she's not the only student who feels this way. In fact, she's thinking about doing a questionnaire around campus for juniors and seniors, but before she does, she wants to get the ok from Mr. Justice. She hasn't talked to Jamal about it just yet, well, not in full detail, but she plans on talking to him on their walk home from school.

But first, she has her meeting with Mr. Justice, and surprisingly, she isn't nervous at all. She walks into his office and says, "what's up Mr. Justice! How is your day going?!"

He responds and says, "seems like you have a lot of energy which is great! My day is going good, thanks for asking. How's your day going?"

She says, "I do have a lot of energy" as she laughs out loud. She continues to say, "I am also having a good day, I do have some stuff on my mind that I would like to share with you, I am feeling overwhelmed about the process to attend college, I don't think I want to. I do love school, but I don't think furthering my education in that way is for me."

Mr. Justice says, "well, I respect your honesty and your understanding of what you want and don't want at this age. It is possible that you might change your mind about college, but if you don't, I don't think it is a bad thing at all. I completely understand how overwhelming the experience can be for everyone involved, from parents to the student to that student's family, etc. Trust yourself and do what is best for you, I think so many times, students do what their parents and family want them to do rather than doing what makes them happy. What do you want to do once high school is over?"

Sabrina says, "thank you Mr. Justice! Hearing you say all of that was helpful, which is going to encourage me to be more confident about talking to my parents about it. But I want to open my own business, my mom and dad own their own businesses. My mom owns a hair salon with twenty employees, and my dad owns three barbershops in Seattle, Washington, with fifty employees. Both of them did not attend college, but to be honest, I never talked to them about why they didn't. I look forward to having that conversation with them. I think it will help me get much more clarity and insight into their lives and entrepreneurs."

Mr. Justice says, "I definitely think you should talk to your parents about their lives after high school and don't be afraid to ask them those tough questions. Ownership is so important for us in the black community. I own three of coffee shops with fifteen employees, all young African Americans, who are either in their final years of high school or in college. I also raise money to provide them with scholarships and teach them the importance of ownership. In fact, a few of them will be in attendance for our leadership class later today.

I think you can pick their brains a little bit and talk to them about how you are feeling, peer to peer conversations can and usually are very helpful. Have you talked to Jamal about any of these feelings?"

Sabrina says, "such a wealth of knowledge and understanding. Thanks again Mr. Justice, I didn't know you owned coffee shops and you also have kids my age working for you, that's amazing in every sense of the word. I want to follow in my mom's footsteps and have my own salon and get into real estate. Jamal wants to do real estate too. Jamal and his best friend Ellis have been wanting to get into real estate since the 6th grade. I haven't told Jamal yet about my future, but I feel good about him being supportive and encouraging. I am going to talk to him about it during our walk home from school. I was thinking about having him there with me when I tell my parents for support. What do you think about that? Do you think that is a good idea or should it be just me and my parents?"

Mr. Justice says, "I am glad you and Jamal have such a strong bond, I love that you guys want to get into real estate. That is one of the best ways to build generational wealth. Your parents being entrepreneurs is amazing, I think that helps you understand the importance of ownership and more specifically, black ownership. I don't think having Jamal there with you when you tell your parents is a bad idea. However, I do think you should tell them first then have Jamal come after, just so you have your parents can have that important and intimate conversation as a family. I think your parents would appreciate that a lot. But that is just my opinion, the choice is ultimately up to you. You seem to have a good judgement and I think you should trust that. You don't need anyone to tell you what you should or shouldn't do, follow your instincts with this situation. You can't go wrong with that." Sabrina smiles and tells him she will see him later during class.

Jamal sees Sabrina leaving from Mr. Justice's office and asks her if everything was alright? Sabrina says, "yes, I just needed to talk to him about this leadership class and a few other things. I will talk to you about it all in detail during our walk home from school today."

Jamal says, "alright sounds good! I look forward to having this conversation."

They have two more classes until they have their leadership class for the last period of the day. Jamal is excited about the school assembly tomorrow morning, where he gets to introduce the new class to help his peers deal with anxiety and stress. No one knows about this assembly, not even Sabrina, but he is going to tell her when they walk home from school. Jamal is so nervous and eager to see his peers and teacher's reactions to not just the new class but the positive energy he thinks it will bring from everyone on campus.

Chapter Nineteen

The moment Jamal and Sabrina has been waiting for, Mr. Justice's leadership class is about to begin, and they want to be the first people there and will make sure they are. They can't recall being this excited about any other class. On the way to the class, Jamal sees Sonya and wants to introduce Sabrina to her. Jamal says, "there's Sonya! Sonya, Sonya, this is my girlfriend Sabrina, Sabrina this is Sonya, the girl I was telling you about earlier."

Sabrina says, "it is nice to meet you. Welcome to our school. How was your first day?"

Sonya says, "it is nice to meet you too, thank you for the warm welcome. My first day is going great, I have met some great students and teachers. I was telling Jamal how much different this school is from my last school in Arizona. Everyone seems to care about everyone, which makes for a great environment. I don't have to worry about any violence, which is something I am so happy about."

Sabrina says, "wow it seems like you had a terrible experience out there. I am glad you moved out here so you could have a different experience and one that is more positive."

Jamal, Sabrina and Sonya walk into their last class of the day with Mr. Justice, the leadership class that they all are excited about and have no idea what to expect. As they walk in, they notice he is not there. They also turn their attention to the projector and see that it says, "good afternoon! Find a seat or stand if you like. Make sure you introduce yourself to at least five people you don't know. Make sure you tell them your first and last name, grade, and why you think you are in this class. I have made sure to include all grade levels, nineth-twelfth."

He also appointed Jamal as the classroom president, which meant, that anytime Mr. Justice would miss a day or would be late to class, he would have Jamal lead the class. Mr. Justice already decided that Jamal would lead the class at least once a week. Despite him not communicating it to Jamal, Mr. Justice saw this as a great opportunity to see how Jamal could lead his peers in a setting where he would be comfortable. Mr. Justice finally walked into the class, he tells Jamal to come up to the front and has him introduce himself to everyone, and he also wanted Jamal to let everyone know about the class he created to help not only his peers but the staff as well. Some students were aware of it, but Mr. Justice wanted to make sure they all were aware.

Mr. Justice pulled Jamal to the side after class and asked him why is school important to him, Jamal said, "it is not that I think highly of school to be honest, but I enjoy connecting with my peers and having the possibility of developing and maintaining relationships. That is what I value about school."

Mr. Justice smiles and says, "I enjoy having conversations with you, you are mature beyond your years. Relationships are the key to life, and I am glad you are able to recognize that."

*****

On the following morning, which was Saturday, Jamal asked Sabrina if she wanted to meet up and get some food. Sabrina who was still sleep realized how early it was and told Jamal she would call him back once she woke up. Once Sabrina called him back, they both talked about how excited they were about their future and how much they appreciated Mr. Justice.

The two meet up and Jamal wanted to ask her some questions to see what her response would be, "what is the biggest lie you've told up yourself to this point of your life?"

Sabrina looks at him with a confused face and says, "that is a great question. The biggest lie I've told myself is, if I ignore something, it will eventually go away. What made you ask me that question?"

Jamal says, "I'm going to ask that question to a plethora of people of different age groups. I am curious to know their answer because I want to learn from them in regard to their life and how they have either hindered themselves or strengthened themselves."

Sabrina says, "what about you?"

Jamal rubs his chin and says, "even though I planned on asking people this question for some reason, I didn't expect to answer it. But the biggest lie I have told myself is, someone would ask me how I am doing, and I would give them a generic answer, like I am doing fine," but deep down I was hurting emotionally. Hurting because I was always under the impression that love is unconditional and for some it might be but for me it seems like when people I thought would always love me such as my family but that couldn't furthest from the truth, even though my dad and I have been able to build a relationship, I'm still confused about why he chose to leave and not return or even try to locate me, I had to locate him, so when I am asked how I am doing that is how I am doing. I am hurt, I blame myself for a lot of things, I could go on and on, but one of my favorite quotes of all time is, this too shall come to pass."

Sabrina looks at Jamal and asks, "do you want a hug? I think you're an amazing person and a person that is destined for greatness. Thank you for inspiring me and encouraging me to step outside of my comfort zone."

Jamal says, "no problem. It is my pleasure to do so. Inspiration comes in different ways. I think you should ask your parents the same question I asked you and see what their answer will be, I can't wait to ask my god mom this question."

*****

During that weekend, Sabrina contemplates asking her parents that pivotal question mainly because she fears what her parents will say and how what they say will affect her. So, she waits a few days before asking the question. Meanwhile, Jamal asks his god mom with no hesitation or fear. He says, "I have a question god mom, what is the biggest lie someone has told you or you have told yourself?"

She says, "what do you mean?"

Jamal says, "I just want some insight on how what you believed to be truly influenced you. I asked Sabrina the same question, and I plan on asking all the people I care about. Gathering up as much information and data I can so that I can continue to be the best man I can be despite any obstacles that may be present. I am on a mission that is bigger than me, and sometimes I have a hard time explaining it."

She says, "well, son, I would love to answer that question. I think the biggest lie I've been told is what unconditional love is and who has it and who gives it. Unconditional love is an active choice to continue loving with no expectations or rewards. I think unconditional love is present with family members, specifically mothers and fathers. However, when it comes to friendships and relationships, from my experience, that most time isn't the case. The reality is most people, love you when you can do something for them, when you can help them in some way shape or form. Even for me, when I would be romantically involved with a man, I would have these unrealistic expectations when it came to them making me happy, I convinced myself that I would always accept them at their best and at their worst when that wasn't true. As soon as I felt someone mistreated me or made me feel less than, my feelings would often change and I would begin to look at that person differently, not to say the love wasn't there but that unconditional love stopped existing. Love is often conditional, in my opinion, as human beings we just don't like to believe that. We don't like to believe it because most of us if not all of us we have been conditioned to think once we love someone there is nothing they can say or do that can change that, but the reality is, that's not true. In closing, unconditional love does exist but is not often present when it comes to people outside of your family, I don't think that is a bad thing though. I just think it is a part of life that we prefer not to discuss in detail because love is such a powerful thing."

Jamal says, "wow, thanks! I completely understand what you are saying. That perspective was amazing and articulated so well. When would you say you came to that realization about unconditional love?"

She says, "I came to that realization when the first man I ever loved broke my heart, he was emotionally abusive, and I often made excuses for him because of my flawed view on love. I saw my mom accept a lot of emotional abuse, I also saw her give it back as well, and if I am being honest, I thought that is what unconditional love was, no matter what anyone says to you or does to you, you continue to put up with it and "stick it out". As I got older, I realized I didn't know how to deal with conflict effectively, I viewed conflict as something that happens and when it does it continues to get ignored by the people involved until it goes away. I think that ties into what I believe unconditional love to represent outside of a family construct."

*****

Once school began the following Monday, Jamal couldn't wait to ask Mr. Justice the same question he asked Sabrina and his god mom. He strolled into Mr. Justice's office and asked him if he could talk to him today after school. Mr. Justice said, "of course, is everything alright?"

Jamal said, "everything is great!"

Once school ended, Jamal raced to Mr. Justice's office because his excitement for having this conversation is unmatched. Jamal walks in and says, "I am ready to ask you these questions. Are you ready to answer them?" As he says with a huge smile on his face.

Mr. Justice says, "yes, I am ready. What's on your mind?"

Jamal says, "well, one of my questions is, what is the biggest lie you have ever been told when it comes to success and the idea of it?"

Mr. Justice says, "that is a great question, let me think about that" Mr. Justice sits there and ponders for about forty-five seconds to a minute. Once he finishes, he answers and says, "I think the biggest misconception when it comes to success is everyone's success is the same, which includes a ton of money. But I think success is about your wealth and not your riches. What I mean by that is success shouldn't be equated to the amount of money you have but instead the number of lives you can affect positively. This is one of the main reasons why I wanted to work with young people, to have a direct effect on the future of our world and to have the opportunity to pour into them regardless of their circumstances. We all need someone to champion us and support us in this thing called life. And I have made a commitment to doing just that. Ms. King did it for me, the least I can do is pay it forward."

Jamal says, "that is a powerful response Mr. Justice and I appreciate your transparency. The reason why I wanted to ask you that question is that I knew you would say something to inspire me, and I am glad I was right about that. Who is Ms. King? If you don't mind me asking."

Mr. Justice says, "I appreciate the question, and I am glad you gave me an opportunity to inspire you. I think that is a huge factor in life that gets undervalued and overlooked, the importance of inspiring your loved ones. Ms. King was my 5th grade English teacher, and she was so patient with me, and kind to me. No matter how I behaved she never got frustrated with me and always, always showed grace. As I got older, I would go back and visit her during every year when I was in high school, I also invited her to my high school graduation and my college graduation. She could do no wrong in my eyes. Shortly after I graduated from college she transitioned and I cried my eyes out for days, and even weeks. After I mourned, her untimely death, I heard a voice say to me, "don't give up, don't ever give up." I think it was her and since then I never looked back. Thank you for listening, Jamal this was like a therapy session that I didn't know I needed. I just hope she is proud of me, and I think she definitely is."

Jamal says, "wow, I can honestly say for this short amount of time that I have known you, I think not only are you making her proud, I have the utmost love and respect for you because you want to see things change and you are supporting that change with actions and not just words. You inspire me Mr. Justice and I will forever be grateful for you; I know I am not the student who feels that way."

Mr. Justice smiles and gives Jamal a handshake and lets him know he will see him tomorrow at school.

Jamal leaves from school and calls Sabrina, he wanted to let her know about his inspiring conversation with Mr. Justice and to also see if she asked her parents the question as well. Sabrina answers the phone and says, "what's up Jamal, how was the conversation with Mr. Justice?"

Jamal says, "it was great! His vulnerability was amazing, and I got to know him on a much different level which inevitably I gained so much more respect for him as a man. Not only did I ask him about his idea on the biggest lie he's been told, but he also talked about his younger days when he was in school, and he mentioned a woman by the name of Ms. King his 5th grade English teacher. A woman who believed in him and how she let him know by her actions she was going to support him no matter what. From that, he understood he had a duty to be to young people what she was to him, a patient, loving, kind, and encouraging role model and one he could always look to for inspiration. He called it paying it forward. I saw so much gratitude in his eyes and when he talked about her passing away shortly after she attended his college graduation, I could tell him either has never said those things out loud or he hasn't done it in a while, and he even called our conversation a therapy session."

Sabrina says, "you never cease to amaze me, Jamal. As for me, I haven't gotten the courage to ask my parents just yet, but I will sooner than later. It seems like my mom and dad are having issues, I don't know what's going on fully, but their energy has been off towards one another. They haven't been spending as much time with one another as they normally do."

Jamal says, "I am sorry to hear that, whatever they are going through, I am sure they will pull through. Is there anything I can do to help?"

Sabrina says, "thank you, you always seem to know exactly what to say and when to say it. I don't need anything other than you continuing to be there for me."

Jamal says, "I will always be here for you."

*****

Jamal finally arrives home from school at 5 pm. His god mom greets him with a hug and a warm smile. She said she wanted to talk to him and to let her know when he was settled in. Jamal was a bit confused and worried. Her tone seemed unsure and hesitate, which he had never heard her that way before. Jamal washed up, finished his homework and walked into her room and said, "did you still want to talk to me?"

She said, "yes, I wanted to talk to you about college, is that something you want to do? I am asking because I know your grandma would've loved for you to get your degree, but I also know the things you are doing for your school, and I wasn't sure if you had college in your plans."

Jamal says, "that's all you wanted? I was nervous" as he says with a smile on his face. I know she would've wanted me to attend college and get my degree. However, I am not sure if that is a route that I want to take, I would much rather go into real estate, start taking classes and building my portfolio. Ownership is on my mind god mom. I love school I just don't see how going to a four-year university, possibly gathering debt is beneficial for what I want to accomplish. I appreciate you asking me and not assuming one way or the other."

She says, "I completely understand. I will always encourage you to do what makes you happy. This is your life, and with all due respect to your grandma, you must live your life for you and no one else. I support whatever you decide to do, my son."

Jamal says, "thank you for being so understanding and supportive; it really means a lot. I had a great talk with my counselor today, and I asked him the same question I asked you, regarding the biggest lie you've ever been told. I am gathering as much perspective I can from whoever I can. His answer was extremely profound, and I gained even more respect and admiration for him."

She says, "that's great, son, continue to shine your light and allow people to inspire you."

Jamal says, "can I talk to you about sex? I have been thinking more and more about it recently, I am still a virgin, but I do want to lose my virginity to Sabrina." Jamal takes a huge sigh of relief, he continues to say, "I am so glad I got that out, it has been really weighing me down to hold that in. I have so many questions, I don't even know where to begin."

She reaches out to hug him and says, "I am glad you felt comfortable enough to let me know how you are feeling regarding your virginity. Let me say it is perfectly normal for you to feel the way you are feeling. I am not a man so I wouldn't be able to fully understand what you are feeling 100%. However, I know this can be a tough part of life for you if you don't have anyone you can open up to. I am going to ask you some questions to get a gauge on how I can help you deal with those feelings productively. I admire your strength and honesty, son."

Jamal says, "thank you for your support! The main thing I struggle with is not knowing how to communicate it with Sabrina, I don't know if she is struggling like I am, but I would be surprised if it doesn't cross her mind. Then I also think about respecting her parents and everything they have sacrificed to be back in her life. It's a range of emotions, I have been wanting to talk to my dad about it, but I thought talking to you about it first would be more beneficial for me. I've watched the movie like "The Notebook", and I want my first time to be special, with someone special, I think I have that in Sabrina. I'm going to see if she is available so I can take her on a date to her favorite burger spot, she loves the milkshakes there. I need to know how she feels about it, if she feels anything or ever has those thoughts, I think knowing one way or the other would help me tremendously. I also struggle with, should I be waiting, should I be married first, just to name a few things, I hear my friends talking about their experiences and it makes me feel left out or scared to say how I feel about it. Peer pressure is something we all face at certain points in our lives and sometimes I feel like I have to succumb to it."

She says, "I hear you and I understand everything you're saying, let me offer this, when you feel those urges or want to act on them, I would recommend you just calling her, allowing her to calm you down without her knowing it. She will feel so empowered, and that would make you guys that much closer without the physical act having to take place. That pressure you feel from your peers is real, but it can only affect you if you let it. Remain in control and only do something because you want too not because you feel pressure from outside people or things. I think you taking her out is a great idea, it will allow you to have a conversation with her about you two as a couple, from the outside looking in, it seems like you guys don't have much time to discuss how you all feel about one another consistently, with all of you guys' extracurricular activities going on outside of school. It is completely fine to be hesitant and worried you are not the only teen who will feel this way and you will not be the last one."

Jamal says, "I am so grateful to have you in my life, I can't say thank you enough for everything. I am also grateful to have Sabrina in my life she really does make me want to be a better person."

Joyce says, "make sure you let her know that I am glad the same way I feel about you is the way you feel about me. Give your girl a call and let her know how you feel. She will really appreciate hearing it."

When Jamal calls Sabrina, he hears loud yelling and screaming in the background. As soon as she answers she says, "hey, I am going to call you right back".

Jamal couldn't help but to feel helpless and confused about

how to best support her without being physically present. Jamal decides to send her a text after deliberating to himself for about ten minutes, he says, "call me back when you get a chance, I heard screaming and yelling in the background, and I wanted to make sure you were alright."

Sabrina texts back and says, "I am fine physically, but emotionally I am struggling; they have been arguing since I got home from school, basically. I am not sure what is going on, but I do plan on asking them. I am just unsure of how to approach that. Thank you for texting me and checking on me. I will call you back when I can. I hope your night is going better than mine. Talk to you later."

Jamal texts back and says, "you were on my mind, and I wanted to call you and let you know. I am sorry you are dealing with that with your parents. I know that can't be easy. Call me back when you can, but you can expect a text from me tomorrow morning, and I look forward to reading your response. Have a good night. I recommend writing down your thoughts so that way it can help you articulate yourself more effectively when you communicate with your parents about whatever issues they may be having."

Sabrina walks into her parents' bedroom and asks her mom, "is everything alright?"

Her mom looks at her and shrugs her shoulders to indicate she doesn't know. Sabrina then asked her if she wanted a hug, her mom nodded her head yes. Her mom put her head in her shoulder and started to cry. Sabrina heard her crying and continued consoling her and squeezing her tighter and tighter. "Mom, where's dad?"

Her mom says, "I am not sure, but he said he would be back later tonight. Things haven't been going as we would hope, but I am confident we will be able to work it all out. Make sure you are continuing to support your dad despite he and I having our issues. Regardless of that, you are still the apple of his eye no matter what."

Sabrina says, "I'm sorry, mom, I knew you guys were having issues, but I didn't know how to ask or talk to you about it. Thank you for opening up to me about it as much as you can. My dad means everything to me, and I am so glad he and I can have that relationship I have always wanted with him. I wouldn't start treating him differently because of the issues you guys are going through. If there is anything I can do to help on any level, please let me know mom. I look forward to seeing you guys' back being affectionate with one another and loving on each other. Seeing that has always made me happy and appreciative for the both of you. I did want to talk to my dad about being more affectionate with me though. More hugs, more kisses, more overall affection."

Her mom says, "I think you should talk to him about his affection towards you, I don't know if he is aware of the amount, you want or need. Your dad is someone I adore and love, I don't think there is anything we could go through that we cannot push through and make it out stronger than before. I am glad you notice the affection he and I show one another, I think it is important for you to see your mom and dad love on one another unapologetically."

Sabrina says, "you guys have laid such a great foundation in this short amount that has shown me what can be and how love can affect your life in a positive way. Jamal constantly shows up for me no matter the situation, he pays attention to me, and it is truly unbelievable at times. In fact, he called me earlier to check on me, he heard you guys yelling and screaming in the background and asked if everything was alright, then once I told him I couldn't talk, he sent me a very comforting text."

Her mom says, "I like Jamal a lot. I can tell he genuinely cares about you and wants the best for you. I am not surprised at all about how he has shown up for you time after time. I know you guys have different things going on with school and just life in general, but I strongly support your relationship with him, and I know your dad does too. Have you guys been able to spend time with one another outside of school?"

Sabrina says, "I am so glad you and dad support Jamal and I that means so much to us. We haven't been able to spend much time with one another, but hopefully we can pick that back up in the upcoming days or weeks. I am going to call him back and see if he has any plans this weekend and if not, we can hang out and enjoy one another."

Her mom says, "yes! I think that would be a great idea and if you want to really make him feel special and appreciated, I think you should plan the whole thing, from the beginning to the end of the date. It would give him the chance to see a different side of you, and more importantly, he can see how thoughtful and caring you are about him."

Sabrina says, "thanks, mom, I am going to do that. That was a great idea as well. We work really good as a team mom" as she says laughing out loud.

Sabrina calls Jamal back and lets him know about the struggles her mom and dad are having, she begins to get emotional, and Jamal says, "it is ok, Sabrina, let it out. Don't hold back your tears, it is cleansing and extremely helpful. If I was there, I would help you wipe all of them."

Sabrina laughs and says, "you are an amazing person Jamal, I can't say that enough. I wanted to call you back and invite you out on a date with me this weekend if you aren't busy."

Jamal says, "wow, really! I was going to do the same exact thing; great minds think alike!"

Sabrina says, "that's pretty cool, I got this though, I'm going to plan our date, it is only fair since you planned our last one."

Jamal says, "I am looking forward to it. I feel good about leaving it in your hands. Now I really have something to look forward to this weekend. What day were you thinking?"

Sabrina says, "let's do Saturday afternoon at 4 pm."

While on the phone Sabrina thinks about driving and if she would be able to learn how before Saturday, which she remembered her dad one day trying to teach her, but she wasn't interested. Now she wants to revisit that and see if she can learn sooner than later. Nothing like a little motivation to change your mind. Now she feels like she has a reason to learn. Jamal stouts through the house and couldn't contain his excitement because his girlfriend is going to plan their next date. He runs into his god moms' room and says, "guess what?!"

She says with a huge smile on her face, "what happened, son?"

Jamal says, "Sabrina and I are going out this Saturday and she said she wanted to plan it. I am so happy and excited! I haven't mentioned to her how I'm feeling regarding what you and I discussed because I wanted to do that in person."

His god mom says, "I think that was a great decision to wait to talk to her about that in person. Do you have any idea what she is going to plan?"

Jamal says, "I have no idea and honestly I don't even want to try and guess, I feel great about it, whatever we do I am just glad I get to do it with her. Completely off topic but when do you think you can teach me how to drive?"

She says, "sounds good, son! You have something great to look forward to this weekend. I can teach you whenever you think you are ready, there's a written test you must take and then the driving test. I suggest reading the drivers book first so you can become familiar with the laws of the road. I can also help you learn to drive after school we can go to empty parking lots. That's how I learned, and I think it was extremely helpful for me as a young girl."

Jamal says, "YES! Thank you! I have been wanting to ask you for a while not, but I didn't know when the right time was to be honest, plus I was always nervous to start because of how difficult it looks. But I am ready now. When can you start teaching me and where can I get that book? We can start on Monday after school and you can print it from the website, DMV.com." Jamal says, "awesome, I will print it off at school on Monday, my goal is to have my license before the summer starts."

She says, "I am going to make sure that happens for you, my son. I am glad you made it a goal of yours. Driving is fun, and I think you'll do just fine."

Jamal doesn't wait until Monday to get started on learning how to drive, in fact, he decided to start one day before on the next day, which was Sunday. As soon as he woke up, he got on his computer at home and began reading the laws of the road.

Chapter Twenty

The following Monday at school, another new student enrolled to their school by the name of Dennis Hillman from Harlem, New York. Jamal and Dennis bumped into one another and that is how they were introduced to one another. Jamal says, "my apologies bro, are you a new student?"

Dennis says, "my fault champ, yes I am. I am looking for my new classroom now. Can you help me?"

Jamal says, "of course! I know how it can be as a new student, let me see your schedule. Oh, you have all the same classes as my girlfriend, Sabrina. I know where all your class are, and you also have the leadership class with Mr. Justice for last period. Dennis, you're going to love this school, in fact, another new student just enrolled a few weeks ago. Her name is Sonya Gillespie, she's from Phoenix, Arizona."

Dennis says, "man, call me DH, all my friends call me that. I appreciate your kindness as I navigate through this new school."

Jamal says, "cool DH! Who did you move out here with?"

Dennis says, "I moved out here with my mom and dad. They have been together since their freshman year in college at Howard University, in Washington D.C. Have you ever heard of it?"

Jamal says, "man that's pretty cool! But naw I have never heard of Howard University."

DH says, "I went on a visit before with my parents, it was amazing! It is a HBCU."

Jamal says, "what is an HBCU?"

DH says, "Historical Black College University, it is about 20 or more of them across the US."

Jamal says, "oh wow! I need to look into that. That sounds very interesting. I would love to talk to you more about that later, if we can. Maybe during lunch, are you able?"

DH says, "for sure we can!"

Dennis walks into class and immediately notices Sabrina, she was sitting at her desk, talking to the person sitting to her right, and had the brightest smile Dennis had ever seen. Dennis had no idea that was Sabrina, Jamal's girlfriend, until a student said her name to ask her a question. Then Dennis sees a seat next to her empty and decides to sit right next to her and introduce himself. "What's up, my name is Dennis Hillman. What's your name?"

Sabrina says, "nice to meet you Dennis, my name is Sabrina. Is this your first day?"

Dennis says, "yes, it is! So far, I am loving this school."

Sabrina laughs and says, "but it is just the first period, not saying this school isn't great but you haven't experienced it all yet but when you do, I do think you will love it, I know I do."

Dennis says, "oh let me explain why I said I love this school. I walked in this class and immediately saw you. You are a beautiful girl."

Sabrina says, "well, thank you, Dennis, I appreciate the compliment."

Dennis says, "no problem."

The teacher walks in and introduces Dennis as the new student, points out Sabrina to be his tutor to help him get caught up with the class and asks to see both after class to make sure they are all on the same page. Sabrina says, "no problem! I will do my best to make sure Dennis is caught up."

Dennis nods his head with a slight smile at Sabrina. When class ends, Dennis asks Sabrina if she could show him to his next class and coincidentally enough, they have the same class. When Dennis asks Sabrina for her phone number, she instantly feels uncomfortable because of her relationship with Jamal and tells Dennis she has a boyfriend and wouldn't feel comfortable giving out her number because it seems like Dennis is interested in her romantically.

Dennis says, "Sabrina, let's exchange numbers so I can make sure I am all caught up in these classes, since we have all of the same classes. What are the odds of that? Seems like fate to me. But I'll digress", as he says sarcastically.

Sabrina says, "fate? I don't think so. More like a coincidence, I am in a relationship and because I care about him and respect him so much, I am going to make sure I communicate with him what is going on before I give you my number, I don't care if it is for school or not."

Dennis says, "I actually met Jamal earlier today and told him a little bit about myself. He seems like a really cool guy, boring but cool. He mentioned he had a girlfriend, but he didn't say a name. But it makes sense to be you. From what I can see you're the most beautiful girl here. He's a lucky guy. A very lucky guy, I must say.

Sabrina says, "thank you for the compliments. But like I said, I am in a relationship with Jamal, and I don't think he would appreciate you flirting with me, especially after he helped you and made you feel welcomed upon your arrival to the school. He's a great guy and I don't like how you think you can sweet talk your way into me liking you, that's not going to happen. I suggest you try that with another girl."

Dennis says, "I love it when a girl plays hard to get, I love a challenge. In fact, I hear you saying how much you care about Jamal and for all I know you might like him a lot, but I am nothing like him and you will see what I mean when I say that as you continue to get to know me."

Sabrina says, "it doesn't seem like you're anything like him, I completely agree with that, this is not me playing hard to get, this is me telling you I am not interested. Can you please respect that?"

Dennis says, "yes, I can respect that for now."

The two walked into class ready to fully focus on their assignments and able to leave their previous conversation outside of class. This Spanish class has been kicking Sabrina's ass, lucky for her Dennis is bilingual and transferred to their school having earned two A's in Spanish from his previous school in New York.

He tells Sabrina, "The way I learned to understand Spanish was I would watch tv in Spanish and turn the subtitles on, sounds strange but it really does help. I also listened to everything I liked in Spanish and before you knew it, I was fluent within 6 months. I also would practice pronouncing words in the mirror. I think you should give that a try and see how that helps you. It's the least I can do since you are helping me get caught up in my other classes."

Sabrina hesitantly says, "thank you, all of that does sound like a great idea. I plan on incorporating it as soon as I get home today. Let the Spanish show watching begin", she says, laughing.

The bell rang for lunch to begin and Sabrina races out to find Jamal so she could give him a big hug and let him know how much she cares about him. She contemplates telling him about her interaction with Dennis because she was fearful that it would cause unnecessary problems. After they embraced Jamal asks, "how's your day going so far?"

Sabrina says, "it is going good, how's your day going?"

Jamal says, "my day is going good as well, your energy seems off, are you sure everything is alright?"

Sabrina looks at him nervously and says, "actually, today, a new student joined the school and was trying to flirt with me during and after class, giving me multiple complements and completely not respecting the fact I have a boyfriend. In one of the classes I was assigned to tutor him and help him get caught up and in Spanish class he actually helped me a lot with his knowledge of it."

Jamal asks, "is his name Dennis?"

She said, "yes, how do you know him?" Jamal says, "I bumped into him in the hallway right before school started and helped him find his classes, and he and I also had a brief conversation about where he moved from and what brought him out here. But I am not surprised that he made a move on you and expressed interest. The reality is, you are a beautiful girl. I don't blame him at all. In fact, I am flattered to be honest."

Sabrina asks, "you're not mad at him? Why do you say flattered?"

Jamal says, "no I am not mad at him at all. I think he is a cool guy. I am flattered because you are who I want to be with and for other people to see value in you like I do is a good thing."

Sabrina says, "oh ok I get it. I am going to exchange phone numbers with him so he and I can schedule us meeting up for our English class. But I didn't want to do that without letting you know."

Sabrina was a bit taken aback by Jamal's response, a part of her was hoping he would be more territorial or jealous. She had that idea based on shows and movies she would watch, and how those movies or shows would express the men of women and vice versa be jealous or inferior to certain interaction their partners would have with the opposite sex. But Jamal was showing her how a confident man represents himself regardless of who meets someone he likes and cares about. He was completely unbothered and unphased. Which naturally provided a certain level of confidence in Sabrina and how she should feel more comfortable with her interactions with other people because school is meant for the students to be social and gain awareness in that field.

Dennis gets home from school and tells his parents all about his day and how exciting it was. He started by talking about Sabrina and how her aura was something he had never experienced before. "Dad, it's this girl in my class, and as soon as I saw her, I felt her energy and just how magnetic she was. Fortunately, our English teacher assigned her to be my tutor so she could help get me caught up in the class. But unfortunately for me, she has a boyfriend, I actually bumped into him in the hallway as I was looking for my class and he was a really nice guy."

His dad says, "well son I am glad you had a great first day and that you were able to meet some cool people. Make sure you respect that fact that she has a boyfriend and don't try to overstep boundaries by flirting with her and trying to have her engage in awkward conversations about your level of interest for her. You always want to respect people and their boundaries."

Dennis says, "well, I already disrespected the boundaries she tried to set if I am being honest, I still tried to flirt with her even after she told me she had a boyfriend."

His dad says, "I see, I would suggest you apologize to her and after that apology make sure you change your behavior towards her. There's nothing worse than an apology being given but it is not followed with changed behavior."

Dennis takes heed to what his dad said and communicated with him that he would apologize to Sabrina for flirting with her.

His dad proceeds to say, "as human beings we are going to make mistakes, but you are defined by what you do after you make the mistake, do you learn from it or do you allow it to continue to control you. I am looking forward to hearing how your apology went with Sabrina tomorrow."

Dennis says, "tomorrow?! I was thinking in a couple of days to give myself time to figure out what I am going to say."

His dad says, "there's no need to wait an extra day, you know you need to apologize, don't procrastinate about doing it. Accept responsibility for your actions and move forward and allow her the opportunity to do the same. Don't make excuses about acknowledging something you know you were wrong about. You always want to evolve as a man and the best way to do that is to address issues right away if you can, and with this situation you can in my opinion."

Dennis says, "you are right dad? I'm just nervous and unsure how she would respond, I hope she takes me seriously and doesn't think I am apologizing just because."

His dad says, "don't give her the opportunity to not take you seriously, when you approach her, look her straight in her eyes and take the apology seriously and I have no doubt she will do the same.

From how you described her she doesn't seem like the type of young lady to hold a grudge or want to walk around campus with any type of negative energy. If you, can it seriously, she will have no choice but to do the same."

Dennis nods his head in the affirmative. "I'll let you know how it goes tomorrow after school. I would love to do it before our first class starts but if I can't, I will do it once our first class is over. I also owe her boyfriend Jamal an apology too because he told me he had a girlfriend named Sabrina and I still flirted with her."

His dad says, "that's great, son, way to take full responsibility for your actions. That's what men do."

*****

The next day at school, Dennis sees Sabrina as soon as he walks into the building and asks if she had a minute to talk so he could apology for flirting with her. Sabrina says, "yes, I do." Dennis looks her in her eyes and says, "I want to apologize to you for how I acted towards you yesterday after you told me you had a boyfriend. I was wrong for flirting with you and I take full responsibility for my actions. That will never happen again. Do you accept my apology?"

Sabrina says, "I appreciate you apologizing and taking full responsibility for your actions. I accept your apology 100%." She smiles and says, "now let's get to class before we are late. Dennis walked into class thinking to himself, wow that was much easier than I ever thought it would be. My dad was right. I am glad to have him as a dad, seriously. The two sit down and Sabrina gives him a note with her phone number on it, that read, "Jamal was 100% supportive of us exchanging phone numbers. Let's get you all caught up."

Dennis reads it, looks at Sabrina and gives her a head nod to indicate how much respect he had for her. Dennis felt so good after apologizing to her because he was able to right his wrong and was going to do whatever it took for him to do that. Next, he had to apologize to Jamal, and he was supremely confident about how that would go. While Dennis was getting a bite to eat during lunch, he saw Jamal sitting by himself and walked over to him and asked if he could join him.

Jamal welcomed him to sit with him, Dennis says, "what's up Jamal, I wanted to apologize to you for disrespecting you and your relationship with Sabrina, I was wrong for flirting with her, I knew she was in a relationship, and I completed disregarded that. It won't happen again; I can assure you of that. I apologized to Sabrina right before class. I wanted to make sure I gave you that same respect and apologized to you. Thank you for hearing me out. Do you accept my apology?"

Jamal says, "I completely understand your attraction to Sabrina and when she told me what happened I wasn't mad or upset. I accept your apology 100% and I thank you for apologizing to both of us. Let's put this beyond us and enjoy the rest of the school year. I have to get to my next class, but I will see you in our leadership class later today."

Dennis walks away very proud of himself and the growth he showed and more importantly, he couldn't wait to talk to his dad about how both apologies went. But before he was able to do that, he wanted to share with the leadership class what happened and walked into Mr. Justice's office to get his permission to discuss what occurred and the importance of apologizing.

Dennis walks into his office and says, "what's up Mr. Justice! I would love to share a story with the class about apologizing today, can I do that? I am extremely proud of myself and want to share that with the rest of the leadership class. I think it would be helpful for them to hear me discuss it, I won't go into too much detail about it, but I want to highlight what the importance of an apology can mean for all parties involved."

Mr. Justice says, "of course you can! That sounds great. I will introduce it as soon as class begins. Way to be a leader, Dennis."

When Dennis walks into class he sees Jamal and Sabrina and walks over to them to let them know he was going to be talking about their situation to demonstrate to the class a positive sigh of leadership that was shown from one classmate to another. Jamal and Sabrina were both in full support of Dennis explaining to the class what happened just one day ago. Mr. Justice walks into the class right after Dennis and lets the class know Dennis wanted to talk to them about an experience he had with other classmates and how that experience helped him and his growth as a young man.

Dennis says, "I appreciate you all giving me the opportunity to talk to you all about an experience I had with a couple of students here at school, I made a mistake, and I took full responsibility for my actions and apologized to both students and moving forward I believe those two students are going to be friends of mine for the rest of my life. I sincerely mean that, those two individuals have great hearts, and I am so thankful to have met both. As you all know I am the newest student here at this school and I was extremely nervous on my first day yesterday, but both welcomed me with open arms and they shouldn't go without being highlighted and celebrated, Jamal and Sabrina you guys are amazing."

The students in the class turn around and look at both and then gave them a standing ovation because they agreed with Dennis about how amazing they both are. One student really took a liking to Dennis, and that student was Sonya, she felt like she could really connect with Dennis because both of them had so much in common, but the main thing was that they were both new students trying to navigate and adapt to new surroundings.

Once class was over, Sonya walks up to Dennis and says, "I really appreciated your speech, you made a mistake, whatever that was and owned it. My dad hasn't even been able to do that."

Dennis says, "thank you, I appreciate that. What is your name?"

She says, "oh my fault" as she laughs out loud. "My name is Sonya, I just checked into this school about three weeks ago, I'm from Arizona."

Dennis says, "nice to meet you, maybe one day I will tell you what happened between Jamal and Sabrina but for now I want to protect the privacy with that situation."

Jamal and Sabrina walks by and sees them talking and Jamal says, "I see you DH!"

Sabrina says, "oh ok I see y'all too." Dennis turns around and gives them both a big smile and a wink, indicating his level of interest towards Sonya.

Dennis asks Sonya, "can I walk you somewhere?"

Sonya says, "my mom is waiting for me in the front of the school, but I can give you my number and you can call me later today."

Dennis says, "that sounds good." Trying to play it cool but deep down he was excited.

Jamal sees him and calls him, "DH, DH, wait up, how did that go?"

Dennis says, "it went really good, I offered to walk her somewhere and she said her mom was waiting for her in the front of the school, but she did give me her number and told me to call her later tonight."

Jamal says, "that's dope bro, are you going to call her later tonight?"

Dennis says, "I definitely will! She had good energy and had a calming presence about her. I really want to explore that and see if we can possibly go out on a date or two. I would love that. She seemed like she was interested in me so we shall see."

Chapter Twenty-One

The weekend has finally arrived, which means it is time for Sabrina to take Jamal out on a date. On Saturday morning, Sabrina asked her mom if she could give her some advice on how to approach the date. With it being a few hours away she was beginning to get a little nervous. But before she asked for that advice, she wanted to talk to her mom about driving and the process of learning.

Sabrina asked her mom, "when can you or dad teach me how to drive?"

Her mom says, "whenever you think you are ready. We can start learning tomorrow if you want to."

Sabrina says, "yes! Tomorrow sounds great! That was easy. Now back to this date, as she says with a smile on her face. I know he's going to enjoy whatever we do but I want to make it special for him."

Her mom says, "I think you should go back to the park he took you to on your first date. He would appreciate that. Let's go set everything up now. I can help you with decorations and make it his favorite colors."

Meanwhile at Jamal's house his god mom is teaching him how to drive. They found a vacant parking lot, Jamal seemed to be struggling at first, mainly because he was nervous and very hesitant but once he was beyond the wheel for about 15 minutes, he confidence slowly began to grow. Before his god mom new it he was rolling through that parking lot with no problems. So much so, he asked her if he could drive them back home, even though it was just around the corner, she said, "no rush son, we have plenty of time for that. For now, let's just focus on mastering this parking lot and then we will worry about driving on the street later down the line once you learn some of the traffic laws."

On the way back home, his god mom asks Jamal, "are you ready for your date with Sabrina?"

Jamal says, "I sure am. No matter what we do or where we go, I am sure we are going to have a good time."

She asks, "how's school going? I haven't asked you that in a while because I always assume everything is going great. But I need to stop assuming that."

Jamal says, "school is going great, a new student started a week ago, his name is Dennis Hillman and he's from New York. He's a very cool guy, he was flirting with Sabrina during their class and apologized to her and me in front of our leadership class earlier today. The reason he apologized was because he felt like he was being disrespectful to her and me, Sabrina was more upset about it than I was. I honestly was offended, nor did I feel disrespected at all, I know she's an attractive girl and I know guys are going to show interest in her."

She says, "that is an amazing perspective to have at your age son, I know grown men who don't have that level of maturity especially when it comes to women, they're interested in. I'm proud of you for handling that with so much understanding and grace. Was Dennis confused or taken aback by how you chose to handle it?"

Jamal says, "I honestly don't think he was taken aback by it. He understood what he did was wrong and wanted to make sure he fixed it. In my opinion, he fixed it. His apology was great. It took a lot of courage for him to do that, and he earned even more respect from Sabrina and I. Not only that, the other new girl in our leadership class expressed some interest in him, I saw them talking after class and it looked like some flirting was going on, he also said he thinks she is interested and that he wanted to explore that by going on a date or two."

She says, "look at that, I love how everything has a way of working out for the good as long as you do good. I am happy for him. But you need to start getting ready for your date, it is almost 3 o'clock."

Jamal says, "true indeed, I am about to start getting ready now."

*****

Sabrina and her mom finish setting up the park and rush back home so she can get ready. She thought everything out except her outfit, so tried on several things and then decides on a blue summer dress, she wanted to be very intentional about wearing his favorite colors and his favorite colors are any type of blue and white. He loves the way those colors look. Sabrina finally gets done getting dressed and asks her mom to take her to pick up Jamal, she calls Jamal, "Jamal, me and my mom are on our way to pick you up, are you ready?"

Jamal says, "I will be ready by the time you get here, I just got out of the shower, but I'll be dressed by the time you and your mom get here."

As Jamal was getting dressed, he sees that Ellis is calling him, he rushes to pick up the phone, "Ellis my boy, WHAT'S UP! Man, I am glad you called, so much for us to catch up on. How's everything going out in Houston?"

Ellis says, "man, it is good to hear your in good spirits, everything here is going great! School is fun, and the girls here actually seem like they like me. I was thinking about coming back out there for our senior year. I think I can make that happen. I miss you guys!"

Jamal says, "that would be dope bro! All of us together for our last year in high school, talk about epic! I am glad the girls out there are taking a liking to you, but you act like that wasn't happening out here" as he laughs out loud. Sabrina is getting ready to come pick me up along with her mom, she planned a date for us today. I will make sure to tell her you said, "hi" and that you miss us. She will appreciate that."

Ellis asks, "how is she doing?"

Jamal says, "she's doing great, man, for real. I am going to fill you in with everything once I get back from this date. She's calling me right now; I'll talk to you later bro."

Jamal walks outside with the biggest smile on his face, enters the car and greets Sabrina and her mom. Good afternoon, ladies. It is good to see you both."

They both say in unison "it is good to see you too, Jamal."

Jamal says, "guess who just called me?! Naw forget guessing, my boy Ellis just called me! He's doing great and wants to come back out here for his senior year. He asked about you and told me he missed us so much."

Sabrina says, "I am glad he is doing good and hopefully he can move back out here so we can all finish high school together."

Jamal says, "yes, that would be a dream come true for both he and I."

Before they approach the park, Sabrina asks Jamal to put a blindfold on, so he doesn't see the surprise she has for him. Jamal happily puts the blindfold on and sits there patiently awaiting their arrival to their destination. He asks Sabrina a rhetorical question, "where are we going?" He wants to know but then again, he doesn't want to know. Because he loves the element of surprise.

Sabrina says, "I'm not telling you; you will see when we get there."

They finally get dropped off at the park, Sabrina removes his blindfold, and Jamal sees a beautiful layout with light blue and dark blue balloons along with some of his favorite snacks, chips, and she even had the local pizza man Mr. Tucker pull up and make them handmade pizzas from scratch. In fact, he thought it would be a better idea if they made their own pizzas from scratch. Jamal asks Sabrina, "what are your favorite toppings on a pizza?"

Sabrina says, "I like mushrooms, sausage, peppers and spinach. What about you?"

Jamal says, "spinach, chicken, jalapeños, and peppers as well. This was a great idea. A pizza-making date, you've outdone yourself Sabrina," as he says with a huge smile on his face.

Mr. Tucker walks off and tells the young couple to enjoy themselves. Jamal says, "I have to tell you something, Sabrina. Nothing is wrong so I don't want you to think that at all. But there has been something on my mind, and I have to talk to you about it."

Sabrina says hesitantly, "alright, I am all ears. What's on your mind?"

Jamal says, "I'm not sure how to say this but I am going to try my best. Are you a virgin?"

Sabrina says, "oh, I didn't expect that, but yes I am."

Jamal says, "I am asking because this is something that has been on my mind for some time now. Wondering if this is something that has been on your mind too, I want to be able to experience you in that way, but I also want to make sure it is something you want as well."

Sabrina says, "I appreciate your honesty, and to be honest it has been something on my mind as well. I would've never acted on it like you just did though", as she says with a smile on her face. She continues to say, "I would like to experience you in that way as well, I don't know when, but I know I want to. Have you told anyone else this?"

Jamal says, "oh, ok I am glad we are on the same page; it could've gotten awkward if we weren't on the same page. Yes, I spoke to my god mom about it, and she was extremely supportive, she encouraged me to talk to you about it. Would you talk to your mom or dad about it?"

Sabrina says, "I am glad you got that support from her and as far as me talking to my parents about it, I am not sure. I would like to, but I also wouldn't know how to be honest with you."

Jamal says, "I think you are my best friend, and I couldn't imagine sharing that experience with anyone else, and I wouldn't want to." Jamal then leans in for a kiss and Sabrina happily obliges.

As the sunsets, Jamal says to Sabrina, "call your mom so we can head home. Thank you for this amazing date. I look forward to telling my god mom all about it."

Sabrina says, "sounds good. I will call her now. I look forward to talking to my mom about it as well. Should be a great conversation," as she laughs out loud.

Jamal asks, "what is so funny?" As he also laughs out loud.

She says, "because I know how my mom is and I know she's going to have some jokes but in a good way."

Jamal says, "yea, I definitely understand. Your mom is hilarious."

When her mom pulls up, Jamal and Sabrina walk to her car holding hands and laughing and smiling at one another, when they enter the car before her mom could ask anything, Jamal says, "we had such a great time! And I heard a special someone helped her with the decorations, and I want to say thank you! Everything was amazing."

Connie says, "I would do that again and again for you guys. I had so much fun planning that with my daughter. I think you guys are amazing. I really do."

After they drop Jamal off back at home, Sabrina asks her mom, "how's dad doing?"

Connie says, "he is doing good. He's home now and is looking forward to hearing all about your date."

Sabrina smiles and says, "I can't wait to talk to him about that and much more, I feel like I haven't had a chance to talk to him in a while."

Connie asks, "what else did you want to talk to him about?"

Sabrina says, "I want to talk to him about you guys' relationship as well, I've been a little concerned with all of the arguing and I feel like it has caused a small wedge between the relationship between he and I."

Connie says, "I didn't know you felt that way, I didn't think it affected you that much. But I am glad you feel confident and secure enough to talk to him about it. I think that is amazing."

The two walk back in the house and see Keith making himself something to eat in the kitchen, Connie greets him with a hug and a kiss, Sabrina then greets him with a hug and asked if she could talk to him after he finished eating.

Keith says, "of course we can talk sweetie. Is everything alright?"

Sabrina says, "I think so, but I just miss you and we haven't spoken in a few weeks, which seems like forever."

Keith says, "I completely understand, I look forward to us sitting down and having a discussion about my actions as of late."

Sabrina says, "sounds good, dad."

Keith goes into his room and asks Connie to follow him so he could get a gauge of what she may have told Sabrina, he wants to make sure they are on the same page. He asks Connie, "did you talk to Sabrina about us?"

Connie says, "no, not really I made sure to keep everything vague just as we discussed. She is going to be crushed, but the sooner she knows the better. You are moving back to Seattle is going to hurt her more than you know. She has always longed for that relationship with you and she's going to feel like it's being taken away. I hope I am wrong, but we shall see."

Keith says, "I know she's going to be devasted, but it is our job to ensure she still feels that love despite us not working out how we thought we would. I am going to talk to her privately, and then I am going to ask you for your support when we tell her about me moving back to Seattle. Are you good with that?"

Connie says, "yes! I think that is a great idea."

*****

Keith is ready to talk to Sabrina, he walks to her room, knocks on the door, and says, "you ready to talk baby girl?"

Sabrina says, "yes dad, come on in. Talk to me dad, how are you doing?"

Keith says, "I am doing good. I know you have heard your mom and I arguing a lot for the past couple of weeks, I apologize about that."

Sabrina says, "yes, I have heard you guys arguing, why have you guys been arguing?"

Keith says, "we just haven't been seeing eye to eye on things that I don't want to speak about right now. I am going to go get your mom now so we can all have a conversation."

Keith walks back to his room and lets Connie know he is ready for her to come join the conversation, before they leave to go back to Sabrina's room, Connie asks Keith, "are you sure we are doing the right thing?"

Keith says, "yes, I think we are."

They walk into Sabrina's room, sits down on her bed, Connie reaches for Sabrina's hands and Keith starts the conversation by saying, "Sabrina, sweetheart, I love you so much and I love how our relationship has grown and flourished over the past few months. Sabrina has a look of confusion and sadness on her face because she was bracing herself for the bad news she knew was ahead. Keith continues to say, "your mom and I have tried to make our relationship work, and unfortunately, we have not been able to successfully work through our differences. That doesn't mean we don't love one another anymore and that doesn't mean we don't love you. What it means is we concluded that the both of us are better off co-parenting with you being the priority to both of us."

Connie adds, "I love your dad dearly, we have discussed this on multiple different occasions prior to us making this decision, we agreed that this is for the best."

Keith says, "I am going to be moving back to Seattle next week. I am still going to make sure I am in communication with you, I am going to make sure I fly you out to visit me as well."

Sabrina looks at both her mom and dad and says, "I completely understand, I appreciate you guys sitting me down and talking to me about this as well. I knew something was off between you two. I just didn't know what it was, but I support both of you 100%. Also, I look forward to coming to visit you in Seattle, dad. I love you both so much."

Her parents look at each other and have the biggest smile, their baby girl is a very mature and understanding young woman and both are extremely proud. Connie looks and Sabrina and says, "we appreciate you so much, I love that perspective and for you to have that outlook on life at this age is incredible."

Keith adds, "I agree with your mom 100%. We are still going to be a happy family and I look forward to creating more memories with two of my favorite ladies."

Sabrina says, "I love you both! Now can we talk about my date with Jamal," as she says with a slight grin on her face.

Keith says, "yes, let's talk about it, we are all ears."

Sabrina says, "so me and mom decorated the same park he took me to for our first date, with balloons of his favorite colors which are shades of blue, then I had Mr. Tucker come and teach us how to make pizzas since that is one of Jamal's favorite foods. As we are making our pizzas, we had such a great open and honest conversation about sex. I want to share that with both of you because I trust you guys enough to feel secure with sharing that information. Jamal was talking to me about how it has been on his mind, I was truthful with him, and I shared with him that, it hasn't been something that has been on my mind a lot, but it has crossed my mind periodically."

Connie gives Sabrina a hug and says, "I can only imagine how hard that was for you to communicate that with us, we have your back. Your dad and I knew we would have to have this conversation sooner or later, my advice to you is this, make sure whatever you do, you are doing it because you want to and not because you feel forced to."

Keith says, "I share those same thoughts and sentiments as your mom and I want to add, remember you are in control of you and no one else. I would love for you to wait until you were a little older but if you do lose your virginity sooner than later, make sure you protect yourself by using a condom. Being as responsible as you can is the key."

Keith gives her a hug and tells her you are going to be just fine, my dear."

Sabrina asks, "when did you two lose your virginity?"

Keith contemplates lying to her and not saying the real age he lost his virginity, but he decided to be honest with her and say the real age, which was seven-teen, and for her mom, coincidentally, it was the same age, and it was to her dad. Sabrina looked at both surprised and excited because they were able to share such a sacred moment with one another at such a young age.

Sabrina said, "you guys are pretty cool, you guys shared that moment way back then, and somehow I got created shortly after, how amazing is that." She says that with the biggest grin on her face.

Connie says, "be careful little girl, as she laughs out loud.

Sabrina says, "well mom, it is true," as she laughs out loud again. Sabrina says, "alright but seriously, I appreciate you guys' advice and I am definitely going to take heed to it. The great thing about all of this is Jamal is a great person and I know he has my back to the fullest. Mom and dad, our sophomore year is almost over, any idea what I should do for the summer?"

Keith rubs his chin and says, "you can come visit me in Seattle for a few weeks, as long as it is aright with your mom."

Connie says, "that is a great idea, we can book the ticket now." Connie was thinking this would be a great time for me to travel as well. Connie says, "I have been wanting to plan a trip with my girlfriends to Jamaica and that would be the perfect time. We both can have ourselves a vacation."

Keith says, "well, there it is. It's going down!" As he does his old man dance, which Sabrina refers to.

Sabrina says, "alright dad, I'll come on one condition, you have to retire that old man dance, at least while I am out there."

Keith says, "not a chance," as he laughs out loud and walks back into his room, with Connie right behind him. They both yell, goodnight, Sabrina. See you in the morning."

Sabrina yells that right back to them, "goodnight mom and dad, see you in the morning." Sabrina looks for her phone so she could call Jamal and let him know about everything that just took place with her mom and dad.

Jamal answers the phone and says, "what's up Sabrina! How are you?"

Sabrina says, "I am doing great! How about you?"

Jamal says, "so am I just getting ready for school tomorrow, I enjoyed our date so much. I can't say enough how much I genuinely enjoyed that."

Sabrina says, "I am glad you enjoyed it, I have so much to tell you, where do I begin. I'll start by saying, my mom and dad just finished talking to me about how their relationship isn't working and that my dad is moving back to Seattle next week. I'll get back to that, I also talked to them about our date and how you mentioned sex, and they were supportive, surprisingly. I asked my parents what they thought I should do for the summer, and my dad mention I should come visit him for a few weeks in Seattle. My mom is going to take a trip with her friends to Jamaica during that time. I know that is a lot to unpack but I wanted to share all of that with you."

Jamal says, "wow, that is a lot to unpack, where should I start? I'll start with you going to visit your dad for the summer, I think that would be great! I support you doing that for sure. When you mentioned us talking about our virginity, what did your parents say? I am beyond curious."

Sabrina says, "I mentioned it, and they trusted me to do it if I wanted to and they both hammered home to me how important it is for me to do it because I want to and not because I am forced. Not that they think you would try to force me, but they were just saying and to also use protection. Safe sex is the best sex. I also asked them when they lost their virginity, and ironically enough, they lost it to one another."

Jamal says, "oh wow, your parents were that candid with you, that is great! I didn't expect that at all, I'm not sure what you expected but I didn't think they would be so supportive, but I am glad they are. I would never force you to have sex with me, and I would for sure make sure I had a condom for protection."

Sabrina says, "I know, my dad was just making sure he explained how important both of those things are for me as a girl."

Jamal says, "I really think the world needs more supportive parents like your mom and dad. Kids our age wouldn't be so lost and damaged. I am glad your dad talked to you about safe sex and protecting yourself."

Sabrina says, "thank you for the kind words, their support really means a lot to me. I am about to get some much-needed sleep, I will see you at school tomorrow and make sure I give you a big hug."

Jamal says, "sounds good, I am sleepy as well. Goodnight, Sabrina."

Chapter Twenty-Two

The following day at school, Jamal sees Dennis walking into the gate at school and yells his name, "DH, DH, wait up, how was your weekend?"

Dennis says, "my weekend was cool, I was able to get caught up on some of my schoolwork. How was your weekend?"

Jamal says, "I am glad you were able to get caught up on some of your schoolwork. My weekend was amazing, I had a great date with Sabrina which she planned the entire thing. We had some the best time. Were you able to talk to Sonya?"

Dennis says, "no, I wasn't able to call her because I was engulfed in my schoolwork, but I want to make sure I talk to her today. As soon as his first period was over, he sends Sonya a text saying, "What's up this is Dennis, where are you?"

She responds back and says, "well, look who finally decides to text me", with a smiley face. I am heading to my next class. Where are you?"

Dennis says, "I am about to walk past the gym, can you meet me there? I want to see you before we go to our next class."

Sonya says, "oh ok! That sounds good to me, be there in less than two minutes."

First thing Dennis says when he sees Sonya is you are so beautiful, I wanted to call you over the weekend, but I was so focused on making up the schoolwork I've missed. But you were definitely on my mind."

Sonya says, "you were on my mind too! I kept looking at my

phone hoping I would get a text or a call from you. But I completely understand you being busy from getting caught up on your schoolwork. Were you able to get caught up?"

Dennis says, "I am glad you were thinking about me that is a good feeling, yes I was able to get caught up on most of it. Can I walk you to class?"

Sonya says, "yes, you definitely can. But I don't want to make you late for your next class."

Dennis says, "don't worry I won't be late."

Sonya says, "alright great!" While Dennis is walking Sonya to class, he is thinking about how he can ask Sonya for a kiss, it seems like they got to her class fast. She leans in for a hug and then he grabs her chin and gives her a peck on her lips. She blushed and said, "thank you, that was a nice kiss."

Dennis walked away feeling like he was on top of the clouds. He couldn't wait to tell Jamal. When Dennis sees Jamal heading to lunch, he stops him breathing heavily and full of excitement, "guess what, I kissed Sonya! I walked her to class, went in for a hug and then went in for a kiss! She likes me, she likes me!"

Jamal says, "man, I am truly happy for you and your happiness! Now you can finally stop flirting with my girlfriend", he says sarcastically. "But seriously that is really cool. Now what is your plan with Sonya?"

Dennis laughs out loud, "yea no more flirting with Sabrina, my plan now is to ask her out on a date, get to know her a little better, and eventually ask her to be my girlfriend. I am going to see if I can walk her home today, maybe get another kiss. Her lips were so soft, even though it was a quick peck, I enjoyed her. But I'll catch you later

Jamal, I am going to call her and see where she is."

Jamal says, "check you out, sounds like you're in love DH and I fully support it. Sabrina and I had a great conversation. She also had a great conversation with her parents, and I am happy about both conversations. Thank you for sharing your experience with a girl you like, more young men and even men for that matter need to be more open with their love and appreciation for women they love."

Dennis says, "I agree with you, maybe you and I can make that cool. I know I won't worry about what others feel about the girl I like, she's amazing and I will make sure she knows that. Let's continue this conversation after school, I have to get to class."

Jamal says, "for sure, let's finish after school."

Dennis walks into his Spanish class and sees Sabrina, gives her a smile and a head nod. Sabrina says, "someone is in a good mood, how's your day going?"

Dennis says, "I am in a good mood, my day is going great, I was able to get caught up on most of my schoolwork over the weekend, Sonya and I are developing feelings for one another, things are going great, I love it out here in Los Angeles."

Sabrina says, "you deserve nothing but the best, I am glad you are receiving it, I like Sonya for you, she's always been really sweet and nice to everyone, she has a genuine soul and she's great to be around. I am rooting for you both."

Dennis says, "thank you, I will make sure to let her know all of that, I know she would appreciate you saying all of that."

Sabrina says, "you know what, I will tell her all of that, as young people we should show each other more love and let people know how we feel about them, it'll be helpful for both of us. I should've told her this a long time ago when she first started at our school, she stood out in a great way in our leadership class by being outspoken and always being respectful within her outspokenness."

Dennis says, "I agree, I think you should tell her all of that. Jamal and I just had a great talk before class started and we are going to finish that talk after school today."

Sabrina says, "that's great! I am glad you guys are having great dialogue, it is so important. I need your help with this Spanish stuff" as she says with a huge smile on her face.

Dennis says, "no problem, I got you! Let's get you an "A". Have you been able to practice at home? Because that is more than half the battle, the more you practice the easier it all becomes."

Sabrina says, "honestly, I haven't been able to practice much, but I will tonight and the next days to come. I am going to structure a plan and stick to it no matter what, I really want to learn Spanish."

Dennis says, "that's good, have a plan and stick to it. Before you know it, you will be fluent in Spanish."

The teacher asks to see both, Sabrina and Dennis after class, he wanted to congratulate both on working well together. He says, "seeing you guys work together has been truly inspiring, so much so, I have talked to my other classes about both of you and your teamwork. Sabrina I am proud of you, continue to push yourself to improve on your Spanish skills." He then asks Dennis to stay and told Sabrina he will see her tomorrow in class. Dennis didn't know what to think, he didn't think he was in trouble, but he still was nervous to see what else his teacher was going to say. The teacher says, "you are a great young man, and this school is so happy to have you, I have been trying to get Sabrina to focus harder on Spanish, but for whatever reason I was unable to encourage her to do so, but you came along and she a totally different student."

Dennis says, "yea sometimes students need that push from their peers instead of their teachers, that has happened to me before too, at my old school in New York. I was having a hard time in my math class, the teacher would try her best to encourage me, I would get help from my fellow classmate and it's like a light bulb went off in my head. Therefore Mr. Justice's leadership class is so successful because he allows the students to learn from one another and he doesn't dominate the class with trying to "teach us" something."

His teacher says, "I completely understand, and I agree. In our next staff meeting, I am going to make sure I communicate that to the other teachers. It will not only make our jobs much easier, but it will also provide confidence to the students as well. Student empowerment is essential to their develop as young people, thanks again Dennis."

Dennis says, "well said, I couldn't agree with you more, students need each other more than teachers realize, and we depend on one another as well. Not just socially but academically as well. Communicating that with the other teachers is an amazing idea and thank you for making that happen. Can you let me know how it goes after you do it?"

He says, "I can definitely let you know how it goes. I appreciate you wanting to know."

Dennis walks to leadership class full of excitement and optimism about his conversation with his Spanish teacher. Even more excitement was on the horizon, Mr. Justice lets the class know that they will be learning about credit and student loans for the next couple of weeks, all the students are aware of both but none of the students have any type of knowledge of either one. Mr. Justice knows how important it is to educate these students as much as he can within these few weeks. He asks, "is anyone aware of what a credit score is or what it means?"

The class looks around and someone yells, "out I am aware of it. I have heard my parents talk about it but to be honest it all in one ear and out the other. They weren't talking to me, so I didn't see the significance in listening for a long period of time."

Mr. Justice says, "the next time you hear them discussing it make sure you are all ears next time. Credit score is essential in today's climate, reason being that it shows institutions that you are responsible financially and aren't in debt which means you owe money. This is Investopedia's definition of credit score"; credit score is a number between 300-850 that depicts a consumer's creditworthiness. The higher the score, the better a borrower looks to potential lenders. A credit score is based on credit history: number of open accounts, total level of debt, and repayment history, and other factors. Lenders use credit scores to evaluate the probability that an individual will repay loans in a timely manner. Make sure you guys write that down and internalize it. My credit score is 800, just to give you an idea and I want you guys to know I am practicing what I preach."

Jamal says, "I'm not going to lie, I think I speak for all of us when I say, I was wondering what your score was Mr. Justice. I am glad you were forthcoming with that information, that is so helpful for us. I can't wait to do my own research when it comes to credit."

Sabrina says, "the more we know about it the more we will understand what to research and how that research will not only point us in the right direction but also provide us with the knowledge we need once we enter the real world. Our next question as a class is, how did you accumulate such a great credit score?"

Mr. Justice says, "that is a great question, I made sure I didn't take out any students loans, what that does is ensure I won't have any debt after college, I financed a car, and I had two credit cards that I only used to purchase gas and groceries. Now all I use is my credit cards for every purchase, except for clothing. I don't know why credit isn't learned about in school, but I am going to change that. Students should not just have an idea of what it is but have a clear understanding of what it is, and my goal is to make that happen for you guys. If you guys ever have any questions about it, let me know, as you all know I have an open-door policy when it comes to any and everything."

Dennis says, "this information is helpful, and I am glad you are introducing this to us before we go to college and go through life not knowing about it."

Mr. Justice says, "I wish I had someone talk to me about credit when I was you guys' age. But not just me, my peers as well, even though my credit is great, my peers suffered because they had no knowledge of what it was. I am a firm believer that, when you know something, you have a different level of responsibility regardless of what it is. And I know this information is beyond valuable."

Dennis says, "I'm going to have a talk with my parents about credit and see what type of information they give me, who else is going to talk to their parents about credit?"

Everyone in the class raises their hands, "this will lead to a great conversation in the coming weeks", Mr. Justice adds. You have a great day, and thank you for having an open mind to this topic."

*****

Dennis gets home and is filled with excitement because of Mr. Justice's leadership class, Everette and Parker, Dennis' mom and dad were both happy to see their son so invested in school. Everette asks, "what brings about the excitement for today my son?"

Dennis says, "Mr. Justice introduced credit and the importance of it today, it was so good, he even told us his credit score which no one in the class expected. Usually, a teacher teaches something and doesn't really give their own personal experience to what they are teaching but not Mr. Justice, he was all in."

Parker smiles and says, "that is amazing, how students were privy to that information?"

Dennis says, "it is 21 of us in that class."

Parker says, "that is great! I wish my high school teachers would've introduced credit to me. Luckily, I educated myself on it pretty quickly."

Everette says, "that is amazing, unlike your mom, I didn't have much knowledge of it and unfortunately I made some huge mistakes in college, getting credit cards I couldn't afford, financing a car I was unable to make timely payments on and not to mention student loans. Mr. Justice is providing a great service for all 21 of you guys."

Dennis says, "I am sorry that happened to you dad, were you able to improve on your credit since then?"

Everette says, "most definitely son, I have a credit score of 765 now, thanks to your moms help and support. I am going to talk to your mom about co-signing a credit card for you, you wouldn't have to make payments on it yet of course but I can make my normal purchase and that will help your credit score significantly. Did Mr. Justice talk to you all about that?"

Dennis says, "that sounds great! No, he hasn't talk to us about that just yet, but I am sure he will in the upcoming weeks."

Parker says, "I think that is a great idea, Everette, lets add him. No need for us to talk in private about that, there's nothing wrong with Dennis hearing us talk about finances and the importance of it. Let's make a point to talk about it more openly with him in fact."

Everette says, "I completely agree, the more he knows the more beneficial it will be for him as he continues to grow and mature into a man."

Dennis says, "I hope my peers have parents like you two, seriously, I love how this conversation evolved into what it evolved into. I went from not knowing much about credit, to now being added to your credit line, this is great! I can't wait to talk to my class about this. Hopefully they all experience similar responses from their parents."

Dennis walks into his room, beaming, full of joy and excitement. Everette and Parker also beam with that same level of joy and excitement, Everette gives Parker a hug and says, "you mean so much to me, we need to have more conversations like that with Dennis."

Parker says, "you mean so much to me as well. And we are going to have more conversations with him about an assortment of different topics. Next topic, I want to talk to him about is girls, I haven't heard much from him about that, but I know my son, I know he has interest in a girl, I can feel it."

Everette looks at her with a look that says, he knows something but isn't going to say it, Parker ignores that look and goes on about how she feels like he is hiding something from her. She feels obligated to get to the bottom of it. Everette just looks at her, smiles and says, "our son is definitely alright."

Parker says, "what do you know that I don't?" Everette says, "just know, you're going to very proud of him. I want you to hear about this from him."

Parker says, "sounds good to me, I remember us having a conversation about how important it was for us to create a safe space for our kids and I am glad we are able to do that. Dennis is such a great big brother to his twin sisters; they adore the hell out of him and vice versa. Every time, he leaves for school Nora and Cora look at me and say, they miss their big brother. They're only five years old and have a pretty good understanding of how to be treated by men they love and care about and let me tell you that is so important."

Everette says, "thank you, I wanted to make a conscious decision to make sure they had a great understanding of that. I know they're going to have their trials and tribulations, but they will have a solid foundation."

Parker says, "I am so proud of you, you are the love of my life, you are the love of their lives, you are simply amazing, in every sense of the word."

Everette gets teary-eyed and then reaches his hands for a hug from his wife and his twin daughters.

Chapter Twenty-Three

Dennis can't wait to return to school so he can talk to the class about his mom and dad adding him to their credit cards, he hopes he can inspire his classmates to ask their parents to do the same thing. On Monday, he contemplates talking to his friends about it before class or just waiting to mention it to the entire class, he decides to wait to mention it to the entire class, but first he wanted to talk to Mr. Justice about it and fill him in on the great news.

Dennis knocks on his door, "Mr. Justice, are you in there?" Dennis found his door closed to be a bit strange because everyone knew Mr. Justice to have an open-door policy with all his students. Dennis knocks and then slowly opens the door, "Mr. Justice, wake up, wake up!" He got no response from him, so he runs out to get help.

As he is running, he calls 911. He ran to his Spanish teacher's classroom since he knew Mr. Yates didn't have a class at that time, "Mr. Yates, I walked into Mr. Justice's office, and he was unconscious, help, help!" Mr. Yates jumps up and runs to Mr. Justice's office, good thing only two minutes had passed, and the paramedics were already there. They were able to wake Mr. Justice and let both Mr. Yates and Dennis know he would be fine. The students see Mr. Justice carted off on a stretcher and was immediately confused and concerned.

Jamal sees Dennis and stares at him with so much confusion, "Dennis says, "good thing, I went to go visit him, who knows how long he would've been in there without anyone knowing."

Jamal says, "oh wow, you went to go visit him?"

Dennis says, "I definitely did, I had some time before I had to head to my next class and wanted to run something by him. Hopefully, he can return before our class starts today. If not, I don't know what we will do."

Jamal says, "I agree but knowing him the way I do, if he is unable to return for any reason, he will definitely have a plan in place."

Dennis says, "I hope you're right." Dennis heads to his next class, heart heavy and just overall uneasy about what he witnessed. But he did not let that stop him from attending the rest of his classes and being fully engaged. He recalled a conversation his dad had with him after his grandma passed away, "I know this is tough for you son, hell it is tough for me too, but it is important for us to push forward, that is what she would've wanted us to do. It is perfectly fine for us to grieve, make sure you allow yourself to feel those emotions and don't run from them."

Even though this situation isn't on the same level as his grandma passing away, he still realized he could take a lot away from what his dad told him. Mainly when he says, "allow yourself to feel whatever emotion you feel and don't run from it." He remembers asking his dad what it meant to grieve, his dad told him to find out what it meant for himself, but he forgot to do so, but he thought right now would be a good time for him to research the word. He goes to the computer, goes to google and types in, "definition of grieve", grieve is to cause suffering.

At that moment, he realized the power of that word, but he couldn't understand why his dad encouraged him to grieve. He wanted to get some clarity and couldn't wait to have that conversation with his dad after school. The principle makes an announcement over the P.A system that Mr. Justice is doing great and was suffering from sleep deprivation. She wanted to address his leadership class separately and let them know that he would be back tomorrow, and he wanted me to let you all know that he is doing just fine, but he needed to take today to get some rest. All his students instantly felt great and looked forward to seeing him tomorrow. But they were confused to what the class today would look like, so she opened the floor for that class to discuss anything that may have been on their mind, but she made it clear they would only be talking to one another and that she would be present but not available for questions. Mr. Justice encouraged her to do that.

All he wanted her to do was record their conversations and see how it would evolve for the last forty-five minutes of class. The students began to talk to finances and how important credit was, a carry-over conversation from the previous day, Jamal asks the class, "what was the main thing you guys took away from that credit conversation yesterday?"

Dennis says, "the main thing I took away was not only is it important for us to understand the value of credit and financial literacy, but it is just as important for us to ask questions and study it on our own as well. Mr. Justice introduced it to us, but it is our job to follow up, whether it be with our parents or on our own."

Sabrina adds, "Dennis is 100% correct, we have to challenge ourselves, regardless of how uncomfortable this topic is to our parents, we have to search for information and be willing to have a level of discomfort with our parents."

Another student says, "well, all of that sounds great, but my reality is I don't have parents I can go to for that information, truthfully I don't know anyone I could go to for that information outside of Mr. Justice."

Dennis says, "you can come to my house and my parents can help you, that won't mind at all. I am glad you spoke up about your lack of resources, but you can use me as a resource for sure! What's your name by the way?"

The student says, "man, that would be awesome! I appreciate that! My name is Justin, but my friends call me JC."

Dennis says, "alright JC and you can call me DH."

The discussion is doing exactly what Mr. Justice wanted it to do, which was create dialogue about how the students can further their financial literacy without having a teacher included. JC as up and comer basketball player at the school was beginning to get notoriety for his skills when he scored thirty-five points against their cross-town rival, Clemons high school. Only a sophomore he began to gain interest from basketball powerhouse college such as: UCLA and USC. Standing at 6'3 inches, he was beginning to see what the game of basketball could do for him and his family. He would practice every day before from 4am-5:30am, then again after school from 4pm-7pm, the coach told him he would open the gym for him anytime. Justin was focused and was determined not to let anything stand in his way of obtaining a basketball scholarship.

*****

The next day, Mr. Justice makes his return to campus, he

wanted to be very transparent about what happened, and he didn't want to minimize or hide anything from his students. After all, he prided himself on being an open book with his students. As the students enter the leadership class, they all were very tense and unsure of how they should react or treat him, they all have so much love and admiration for him they wanted to proceed with caution and make sure he knew they had his full support.

All the students enter the classroom and take their seats for the day, Sonya stands up and says, "can I say something?"

Mr. Justice says, "of course you can."

Sonya says, "it is so great to have to back, I know I speak for everyone when I say, the school always has a much better energy when you're here, that one day you were gone felt like an eternity. We are all glad you are feeling better and able to return back to school."

All the of students look at her and nod their heads and smile because they agreed with every word she uttered.

Mr. Justice says, "Sonya, thank you for those kind words. I want to talk to you all about what happened with me and why I had to be rushed to the hospital. But before I do that, I want to send my deepest gratitude and love to all the doctors and nurses at that hospital they all were wonderful. What happened to me can happen to anyone, I don't want to minimize what happened, but I was sleep-deprived, something that I hope to get a better handle on, but it wasn't as bad as I thought, and I don't want you all to be overly concerned either. I am committed to making sure I have a better sleeping schedule, and I also will make sure I am staying hydrated and drinking the adequate amount of water per day. I want to give you guys some praise, I heard the recording of you guys in yesterday's class talking, you guys were inspiring, and I was so proud of you all. Does anyone have any questions, comments or concerns about anything?"

In Mr. Justice's class, if students have a comment or question, instead of raising their hands they stand and is encouraged to maintain eye-contact with whoever they are addressing. Dennis stands and says, "I would like to talk to the class about a conversation I had with my parents about credit and the importance of it. I talked to them about the lesson you gave, and it inspired them to add me to their credit cards so I can start building my credit now. I had no idea that me mentioning the lesson from you would encourage them to add me to their credit, but I am excited and looking forward to how it helps and empowers me."

Mr. Justice says, "that is awesome! I am glad your parents decided to do that for you! You will see the benefits of it when you start using your credit. I encourage all your parents to do that if they can. The value of that is truly priceless."

Sabrina stands up and says, "wow! That is amazing, Dennis. I am going to talk to my parents about doing that as well and see what their thoughts are. Thank you for sharing that with the class."

As class ends, Sabrina asks if she could speak to Mr. Justice about something important. Of course, he says he can talk to her.

Sabrina says, "first things first, I know we already addressed you being absent, but I can't reiterate enough how happy we all are to have you back. I want to talk to you about the situation with my parents, they are separating, and it wasn't bothering me at first but as the days get closer and closer to my dad moving back to Seattle it is beginning to weigh on me heavily. I need some advice on how to proceed, do I continue to act like it doesn't affect me or do I communicate that it does? I don't want to confuse them, but I do want them to know how I honestly feel at this point."

Mr. Justice says, "as a human being you have a right to change your mind or for something to change your mind, it is not out of the realm of possibility that initially when you heard they were separating it didn't affect you like it does now, I think your parents would be very understanding and would be more than happy to hear your honest opinion versus one that you thought they wanted to hear. I think that does much more harm than good, especially with a situation like this, I want to encourage you to not be afraid of your feelings and to not try to hide them no matter the situation or circumstance. You owe it to yourself to say how this really makes you feel, not only will they understand but they will appreciate you for being honest and transparent with them."

Sabrina says, "thank you! I needed to hear all of that, I was struggling with my feelings and wasn't sure how to address it with them or even with myself. They deserve to know how I really feel, and I am going to make sure I let them know. I don't know when I am going to do it, but I need to do it soon because my dad moves back to Seattle next week."

Mr. Justice says, "in my opinion there's no need to prolong the inevitable, do it today when you get home, don't waste any more time. You can do this! And when you do I look forward to hearing how great it went."

Sabrina asks, "what does it mean to prolong the inevitable?"

Mr. Justice responds and says, "basically it means, not to wait on doing something that is bound to happen."

Sabrina says, "thank you for that definition, that is a phrase I am going to start using."

Chapter Twenty-Four

Connie picks Sabrina up from school and notices her energy is a bit off, she asks her, "how was your day at school?"

Sabrina says, "I had a good day overall, mom. How was your day?"

Connie says, "I had a good day overall as well, is there anything on your mind?"

Sabrina says, "there is something on my mind, mom, I am just having a hard time opening up about it, but I did have a very productive conversation with Mr. Justice about it and he was able to help me gain more confidence in being about to talk about it."

Connie says, "well, I am glad you had someone to get advice from, whenever you want to talk about whatever it is, I'll be more than happy to listen."

Sabrina says, "thanks mom! I want to talk to you and dad about it and I think having both of you present would be beneficial."

Connie is a bit confused because she doesn't know what is on Sabrina's mind and for her to want to have her dad present as well is throwing Connie off. Connie rubs her chin and says, "I will make sure your dad can be present, do you want to have this conversation now?"

Sabrina says, "yes mom, it is no need to prolong the inevitable." Connie and Sabrina walk into the house and look for Keith, they find him working in his office. Sabrina says, "hey dad, do you have a minute for us all to talk?"

Keith says, "of course, baby girl, I always have time to talk to you."

Sabrina says, "I wanted to talk to you both about my feelings towards dad moving back to Seattle, I wasn't fully honest about how it is affecting me, initially finding the information I was fine, but as time is going by and it comes closer and closer for him to move back, I am struggling with it. Struggling because I am confused about what happened between you guys, everything seemed fine and then I looked up and now it is not. I need answers from my parents, I know that would be helpful for me to cope with what is happening. You guys being secretive and keeping it from me doesn't help me at all, I don't know why you guys chose to keep it from me, but I really need you guys to explain to me why my dad is moving back to Seattle."

Connie looks at Keith, smiles and says, "she's right, we need to talk to her about why you and I are separating, do you want to explain it to her or should I?"

Keith says, "we both can explain it to her, Sabrina, thank you for opening up to us about your feelings and I am glad you asked us to talk to you about it, your mother and I are separating because we realized that we are better off as co-parents and not being in a romantic relationship."

Connie adds, "your dad and I will always be best friends and we will always want the best for one another, just because we didn't work out doesn't mean we hate each other or despise one another. We realized for us to be the best versions of ourselves for you, it is best for us to co-parent."

Sabrina looks at her mom and says, "thank you for that explanation, it makes a lot of sense, I would hear you guys arguing a lot and I never understood why, this is the clarity I needed from both of you. Being able to have dialogue like this will only make our family stronger."

Keith and Connie nod their heads to agree. They admire their daughter's maturity and understanding of who she is growing to be as a young woman. They walked out of her room feeling like a weight has been lifted off their shoulders. They were able to have a difficult conversation with their daughter and it end on a positive note. Sabrina lays on her bed looking up at the ceiling, thinking to herself, that was such an easy and free-flowing conversation, I almost didn't have it but luckily for Mr. Justice he motivated me and inspired me to have it. I can't wait to talk to him about this tomorrow.

She has one more thing to mention to her parents, she walks into their room and says, "I know I said this already, but I really value that conversation we just had, I look forward to us continuing to have conversations like that to make our family strong. Goodnight mom and dad."

*****

The next day at school, Sabrina couldn't wait to get dropped off at school so she could talk to Mr. Justice, she knocked on his door, "Mr. Justice, do you have a minute? I want to talk to you about the conversation I finally had with my parents, it went to great."

Mr. Justice says, "of course! I want to hear all about it."

Sabrina says, "I told them how it made me feel and they were so supportive and understanding, I wanted them to explain to me why they were separating, and they did so with no hesitation or fear. They applauded my level of maturity and everything. All in all, it was a great conversation, thank you for encouraging me to have it."

Mr. Justice says, "no problem, I knew you could do it and I also knew once you did it would be much easier than you thought it would be."

Mr. Justice sees Jamal in the hallway and asks, "Jamal, do you know how to play chess?"

Jamal says, "no, but I have heard of the game, just never played. Why?"

Mr. Justice says, "I think you would benefit a lot from learning how to play, I think it is the ultimate thinking game. It requires patience, understanding of each piece, and so much more. I would love to teach you how to play."

Jamal says, "that's great! I think with everything you mentioned it would be much more beneficial if everyone in your leadership class knew how to play. Not sure how my classmates would feel about it, but it would be irresponsible of me to not encourage that."

Mr. Justice says, "you are absolutely right! My apologies for alienating your classmates, that was irresponsible of me! I will introduce it to the class and see what their response is and see how open they are to the idea of playing and learning the beautiful game of chess."

Jamal says, "I am looking forward to this, I think they would relish in this moment of learning the game. I am going to do some research on it before class starts today." Jamal sees Justin sitting on the bench by the gym and says, "what's Justin! How's it going?"

Justin says, "aw brother, no one calls me Justin, call me J.C. Everything is going good, just relaxing and chilling before my next class, we have a big game today, the scouts from UCLA, USC and

Arizona are going to be at the game today. I must show up and put on a show. But I am feeling the pressure I must say, I am excited and nervous. I believe in my talents and my abilities, but you just never know."

Jamal says, "my bad J.C, you got this bro, once you get on the court and you can lock in, you'll be just fine, you've been doing this your whole life, today's game is nothing different. Which one of those schools do you want to attend?"

Justin says, "thanks man, you are cool dude. I needed to hear those words; I would like to attend UCLA. This game will ensure that. They've been recruiting me since I was in the 8th grade. That is my dream school. They also have an amazing psychology program."

Jamal says, "I love that! What is psychology?"

Justin says, "psychology is the study of the human mind and its functions, especially those affecting behavior in a given context. Have you given any thought to what you would like to study when you attend college?"

Jamal says, "that sounds interesting, how did you hear about that? But as for me, I have not given any thought to that, I'm not actually sure if I want to attend college."

Justin says, "well, if you ever want to talk about it, we can. I understand the hesitation. As for me, I am following my passion which is basketball, God has gifted me with this talent, and I can't afford to throw it away. People are counting on me, and failure is not an option. I appreciate the talk; I am going to head to class now."

Jamal says, "good talk bro, I am rooting for you and your future success with basketball. I need to come see you play, as a matter of a fact, I am going to see if everyone in our class can come to the game. Seeing that support from your peers can go a long way."

Justin says, "man, that would be great! It would be great seeing you all there to support. It may even help my nerves and allow me to calm down and relax. Hopefully, some if not all of you guys can make it."

Jamal says, "look forward to seeing us there, you need us, and we will be there. I'll make an announcement today in class. Has Mr. Justice ever been to any of your games?"

Justin says, "yes, he has been to countless games, which I have always appreciated."

Jamal says, "I am glad to hear that. Hopefully we can get him to come with us tonight."

Jamal asks, "have you ever played chess before?"

Justin says, "yes, I have. I am not good at it, but it is a game I was told I should practice. It's a great game to strengthen your mind and patience. Why do you ask? Do you play?"

Jamal says, "Mr. Justice told me I should learn how to play, and I was curious to see if you knew how to play. He plans on teaching us all how to play and he's going to introduce that for today's class. This should be interesting and fun. I have something else to challenge myself with."

Justin says, "that's great! I look forward to him teaching us, hopefully everyone in the class is receptive to it, but even if they aren't Mr. Justice isn't going to force anyone to learn, which we all appreciate."

Jamal says, "I agree! Class is about to start, and I don't want us to be late, see you later in leadership class bro."

Later that day, Mr. Justice talks to the class about chess and the importance of it, he asks the class to stand up if they have ever played, several people stand, then he asks the class to keep standing if you think you are good at it. Surprisingly, the same several students continued to stand. So, he then asks those students, if they wanted to play against each other. The students all agreed to just that. Meanwhile, he wanted to put his focus on the other students that weren't familiar with the game and how to play it.

Of course, he found himself answering multiple questions, so what he decided to do was have the students research the game via the internet and once they were able to ask at least 7 questions based off what they researched he would answer their questions. What that did was allow them to see the importance of the game, see why each piece was important, see how each piece moved, some students even researched the origin of the game. He then asked those students to explain what they thought the most important piece was and why. Meanwhile, he went to go check in on the other students who already knew how to play, he saw some interesting games taking place and gave some pointers to some students to help them see the board a little different.

Some of the students were growing frustrated because he was helping other students win and was taking bragging rights away from others, but he told them right after, "it is not about winning, it is about understanding what you are doing and why you are doing it. As you all get more comfortable with playing then it can be about winning. Chess isn't about winning as much as it is about patience and thinking ahead, for beginners. When I play family members or friends, I can honestly say, it is about winning because of the grasp of understanding me and my opponent have. Chess is the ultimate thinking game in my opinion, if you can master your thoughts, you can master anything. As you guys get older that quote will make much more sense. Today, we discussed the importance of chess and for some of us you guys researched each piece and why they are important. I am so happy you guys are all invested in the game, it will be extremely beneficial for you guys as you grow and develop as young people. Tonight, our very own, Justin Campbell, will be playing his last home high game tonight against our rival school, if you guys can make it out to support, please do so. I will be there and if you are able to attend you won't have to worry about paying, I will get you in the game for free as well as provide you with some nachos and a drink.

Sabrina says, "I would love to come and support you, Justin." Several other students also agreed to going to his last game to support.

Justin stands up and says, "I really appreciate all of you guys, hopefully I am able to get a scholarship offer from UCLA or USC both head coaches will be at tonight's game. I really want to attend UCLA but as long as I can get a scholarship so my mom won't have to worry about how my education will be paid for, I will be just fine."

Mr. Justice says, "you will get exactly what you deserve and much more. Any one of those schools will be happy to have you, they're not only getting a great athlete, but an amazing human being."

Justin says, "thank you Mr. Justice, you have been a great role model and a man I have an unlimited amount of love and respect for, I am going to miss you as well as all of my classmates."

Jamal says, "we are going to miss you too! Please come back

and visit us when you can, we would really love to hear about your college experience."

Justin says, "I definitely will come back and visit you guys, I won't be that far at all. Both schools are close to LA just in opposite directions. Well, USC is in in the heart of LA, not too far from downtown."

Dennis says, "you got this, champ! We will be front row cheering you on. Do what you have been born to do! I am looking forward to being inspired by your performance later today.

*****

As expected, Justin scores a school record 42 points, 8 assists and grabs 9 rebounds, his school wins in great game that came down to the wire 85-84. On his last game playing at his high school, he not only set a school record, but he also made sure he locked up a scholarship offer from UCLA. After the game the head coach from UCLA wanted to make sure he introduced himself to Justin and congratulated him on putting on an amazing performance in front of his home crowd.

The UCLA coach also whispered in his ear, "that is how Bruins compete, awesome job son!" The coach from USC also made his way to Justin and said, "we would love to have you join our team on a full scholarship!"

Justin went from being unsure if he would even receive a scholarship offer to now having two. He was in total disbelief and extremely proud of himself for playing the best he could. He was so locked in on the game he didn't realize he broke the previous record which was 38 points scored by an all American in 1989. During his interview with the local high school sports broadcast, the interviewer asked him which college he would be attending next year, and he answered with no hesitation, "I will be a Bruin next year."

The interviewer says, "well there you have it ladies and gentlemen, Justin Campbell will be attending UCLA next fall. You heard it here first." Justin greets his classmates on his way out of the gym and immediately cries tears of joy as he walks to Mr. Justice, and they hug it out.

Mr. Justice says, "you did it, you did it! You made us all extremely proud tonight. You put on an absolute show son. How do you feel?"

Justin says, "I feel like I just secured my future! And I can't believe it."

Mr. Justice says, "have you decided which school you're going to attend?"

Justin says, "UCLA has always been my first choice, I will be a bruin. The Coach officially offered me a scholarship tonight and I plan on signing my letter of intent tomorrow morning, thank you for everything, Mr. Justice. You truly are an inspiration, and you deserve all of your flowers."

Mr. Justice says, "thank you, I know you're going to excel at the next level and remember I will always be here for you for anything."

Justin talks to his classmates for another five or ten minutes and then he goes back to his locker room, where he received the game ball and showered with his teammates emptying water bottles on him to celebrate his historic night. His high school was in tears talking about how much he enjoyed coaching him for the past three years and how great he would do on the next level.

Justin says, "I appreciate you for everything coach, you believed in me when at times I didn't believe in myself. To my teammates, you guys will always hold a special place in my heart, we have been through it all. Even though we didn't make the playoffs, we fought and had an amazing season, I look forward to coming back and seeing you guys give your all-next year. I can't say thank you enough to each one of you. I didn't just break this record by myself, if it wasn't for us working as a team, it couldn't have been possible, I am truly humbled and appreciative for this day, I will never forget it. I am going to walk home with my head held high knowing how great you guys have been and knowing I was able to reach my goal in with receiving an athletic scholarship from UCLA."

His teammates start chanting, "UCLA, UCLA, UCLA."

Jamal yells, "we are beyond proud of you, Justin."

Justin says, "I love this school and I will miss everything about it. I am about to head home, and I will see you guys bright and early Monday morning. I'm going to UCLA, what a dream come true."

Mr. Justice asks Justin if he wanted a ride home. Justin says, "no thanks, I am going to enjoy this walk home, tonight was a great night, and I don't want it to end at all."

Mr. Justice says, "well, let's go celebrate, we can go get some ice cream, pizza, or whatever you want."

Justin says, "it's alright! I will take you up on that offer another time, I need to get me some rest, I am exhausted. Tonight, has been a night I will never forget, I can't say that enough."

Justin takes a shower in his team locker room; let's his

teammates know he will see them on Monday and begins his walk home. As he is walking, he notices it is significantly darker outside than usual. Despite that he continues to walk and stops at a store to get a water, the store clerk shows him so much love and respect for the performance he put on during his final high school game. Justin walks out of the store and for some reason he didn't want to walk all the way to the light to cross the street, so he walked through an intersection when no cars were coming.

As Justin was crossing the street, he dropped his phone, and as he was picking it up, he got hit by a car going 60 MPH. Because of the dense fog, the car could not see Justin at all. Once the car realized he hit someone he immediately pulled over, ran over to see how he could help, he checked his pulse and realized the young man was not breathing, so he frantically called 911. The driver was yelling out, "help, help, I need help. He is not breathing. The store clerk hears the man calling for help and immediately rushed outside to see what was going on, when he realized who was hit, he dropped his head, let the driver know who the young man was and couldn't hold back his tears. Both the driver and store clerk, waited for the ambulance to arrive, they pronounced Justin Campbell dead at the scene. The police also arrived and asked the driver several questions, the police then drove to Justin's house to let his mom know what just transpired.

The police knock on her door, "Ms. Campbell, are you home? This is the police. We have to talk to you about your son."

She wakes up out of her sleep, "come on in, what's going on, officer?"

The officer says, "can we sit down, Ms. Campbell."

She says, "of course."

The officer proceeds to tell Ms. Campbell her son, Justin had been hit by a car while crossing the street. At that time, she became overwhelmed with emotion and began to tune the officer out, and everything just became a blur, the officer then let her know he did not make it, the impact from the car driving 60 MPH was too fast for him to make it. Unfortunately, he was announced dead on the scene. Ms. Campbell in complete shock, could not believe what the officer had told her, she yelled and screamed and didn't know what to do or say. The police officer gave her a hug and then asked her to come with him so she could identify the body, she stared into space and asked if she could ask his mentor, Mr. Justice to accompany her, the officer says, "yes, that is perfectly fine, I am so sorry."

Ms. Campbell calls Mr. Justice, when he answers she couldn't contain her sadness, "Mr. Justice, Justin got hit by a car and died, he's gone, he's not coming back. Can you come to my house and ride with me to identify his body?"

Mr. Justice wipes his eyes and says, "wait, slow down, what happened to Justin?"

Ms. Campbell repeats what she just said again. Mr. Justice says, "I am on my way to your house right now."

Mr. Justice races to her house, sees the police cars parked and realized Justin was in trouble, her saying he passed away still didn't fully register in his mind. Mr. Justice walks in and sees Ms. Campbell crying uncontrollably in the living on her floor, the police officer is doing his best to console her but as you can probably imagine it is nothing anyone can do to stop that pain she is feeling. Mr. Justice picks her up, holds her and says, I am here for you."

They go to identify Justin and as you would expect Ms.

Campbell is shaking uncontrollably, she is in complete disbelief. Mr. Justice is in the car, thinking to himself, how could this have happened and why did this happen, how was he was going to tell his classmates. Once they identify the body, neither one of them could contain their emotions, they saw Justin and immediately broke down.

The following Monday at school, some of the students had heard what happened to Justin but surprisingly, none of his classmates knew what happened, Mr. Justice struggled with the thought of having to tell them what happened, especially after they all were able to attend his last game and spend that time with him after, Justin was in such a great space, mentally, physically and emotionally. Class starts and by this time all his classmates were aware of what took place after the game and the room was in complete silence and just disbelief.

Mr. Justice says, "I know we are all hurting right now, in this time of confusion, it is important for us to lean on one another, support one another and do our very best to make sure Justin Campbell's name forever lives on. I had the pleasure of spending some time with his mom and she is doing the best she can at this time. I know this is tough, I know this was unexpected on every level. But if I feel like I knew Justin well and I know he wouldn't want us to dwell on this and allow this tragedy to discourage us from doing the great things we are doing. If he was here, he would say, we must continue, despite how tough it is. Justin has the pleasure of watching over us all and I have no doubt he is doing just that. When a loved one transitions, it often leaves the family members and friends confused. But one thing I have learned while living on this beautiful earth is, nothing happens by mistake or happens randomly despite how we might individually feel. Justin lived a life that we will never forget, Justin lived a life that inspired everyone he came across, Justin was on his way to UCLA on a full basketball scholarship, Justin was a hero to us all, fly high champ, fly high. We loved him while he was here, and he loved us. Life is still going to be beautiful."

As the students prepare for their junior year of high school to be over, they all feel empowered and ready to see what their last year in high school will look like, senior year is what most high school students look forward to. It is like a rite of passage; you begin to look at your future in a different way. Jamal, Sabrina, Dennis and Sonya wanted to do a tribute for Justin and wanted to make sure they had the blessing of his mom before they proceeded. They felt like since a month had passed his mom would be more receptive to allow his friends to remember him in a way where the entire school could show up and shower his mom with love.

To end their junior year in high school they knew how important it was for them to make sure the tribute was not only memorable but truly showed Justin exactly how he was. The students spoke to his mom to make sure they had her permission to celebrate her son and they wanted to make sure she approved before they made any moves towards making it happen. The students plan to have the event in the next couple of weeks during their lunch. Ms. Campbell happily approved this event and can't wait to see how the students put it all together. Sabrina asked her for some childhood pictures so they can include them in the tribute. Everyone has their job, Jamal will be the host, Sabrina is the event planner, Dennis oversees the music and Sonya oversees the slide show. Mr. Justice has been appointed to check everything once the students have completed everything.

They are also using his classroom to practice their

presentation. They feel the pressure and are excited to bring this presentation to life. They also wanted to make sure they had a videographer to record the event so they all could look back and watch it from time to time, they made a flyer and posted it around the school to see if they had anyone interested in recording the event and of course they had several students interested. They wanted to make the hiring process simple and easy and with Mr. Justice's help they quickly decided. They hired a 9th grader by the name of Luke Jackson. They were all so impressed by him. He exuded a level of confidence that made their decision that much easier. Honoring their late friend is something they can't wait to do, now that they have everything in place, they are ready to celebrate him in a way that will not only bring the school closer but to acknowledge a life that was valuable to everyone who knew him or met him.

Jamal and the team made sure to post flyers all around the school and the neighborhood, they knew the impact he had to the people in that community. He was an inspiration. UCLA coaches also wanted to make sure they came down to show their support, they emailed Mr. Justice and let him know they would be coming down on that special day. A day they call, "Justin Day". Which is a day that will always be celebrated in some way shape or form even when his classmates are no longer at the school, his legacy will live on. They were so nervous and excited because they were unsure about how many people would show up and support.

Mr. Justice was there about an hour early and began to see the amount of people standing in line waiting to be let in. He immediately called Jamal and said, "you guys have to get down here! This is amazing."

Jamal said, "we are on our way, I love the amount of excitement in your voice Mr. Justice. We must execute this for Justin, I know he is smiling down on us loving this! Are you ready to give your speech? I can't wait to hear it. I know you're going to represent him in a way that only you can."

Mr. Justice says, "I am definitely ready to give our speech, I am going to touch the souls of the people that knew him and those that didn't are going to wish they had the pleasure of meeting him."

Jamal introduces Mr. Justice to everyone in attendance, which is 215 people, Jamal says, "I am now going to bring up our very own Mr. Justice, he had the pleasure of having one of the strongest relationships with Justin and he is going to shed some light on the wonderful life of our classmate and friend. Take it away Mr. Justice."

"Good afternoon loved ones, today we are here to celebrate the life of an amazing young man. A young man that brought great value into the lives of the people he touched. His energy was infectious, I had the pleasure of teaching him for this past year as it is my first year here at this wonderful school. He inspired me in so many ways, he encouraged me in so many ways, I am so glad myself and his classmates were able to see his last high school basketball game. He put on an absolute show. Life is so beautiful to me, before the universe decided it was his time to part ways with us, the universe allowed us that great moment with him. He was able to do the one thing he loved at the highest level, which was play basketball, he was on his way to his dream school of UCLA. He left this earth and inspired his peers, inspired me and inspired his family members, and to me that is what life is about. May I ask everyone to stand, this is to love, LOVE."

THE END

Love your loved ones and let them love you.

www.ingramcontent.com/pod-product-compliance
Lightning Source LLC
Chambersburg PA
CBHW061146120626
46546CB00005B/1948